A Kangaroo Loose in Scotland

A Kangaroo Loose in Scotland

One Memorable Summer

Lachlan Ness

ISBN: Softcover   978-1-5434-0621-4
               eBook   978-1-5434-0620-7

Scripture taken from THE HOLY BIBLE, NEW INTERNATIONAL VERSION®. Copyright (c) 1973, 1978, 1984 by International Bible Society. Used by permission of Zondervan Publishing House. All rights reserved.

The 'NIV' and 'New International Version' trademarks are registered in the United States Patent and Trademark Office by International Bible Society. Use of either trademark requires the permission of International Bible Society.

Any people depicted in stock imagery provided by Thinkstock are models, and such images are being used for illustrative purposes only.
Certain stock imagery © Thinkstock.

Print information available on the last page.

Cover artwork by Helen Marshall

Rev. date: 01/18/2018

To order additional copies of this book, contact:
Xlibris
1-800-455-039
www.Xlibris.com.au
Orders@Xlibris.com.au
771352

CONTENTS

For our grandchildren, Laura, Robert, Eleanor and Anna

with love

Foreword

My first two books have in their titles a reference to "A Kangaroo Loose". The first edition of this third book was titled a little differently: "One Memorable Summer" for I thought a change was needed.

While working with Xlibris the publishers, on this current (second) edition, it was decided to return to "A Kangaroo Loose" in the title; hence, "A Kangaroo Loose in Scotland" while retaining "One Memorable Summer" as a subtitle, which means we have a "Kangaroo Loose" trilogy.

We also changed the cover – and I must say I love the new cover, which was designed by that very talented artist, Helen Marshall, who has designed so many book covers; both for me and for other writers.

The original story is much the same, but there is an addition of a lovely poem at the end: "The Banks of the Burn of the Strath of Dunbeath".

I hope you enjoy this wonderful story of our adventures in Caithness, in the North-East Highlands; mainland Scotland's most northerly county.

I know that all those folk in our parish in Caithness who came to mean so much to us will live on in our memories through the pages of this book, as well as in my diaries and letters, just as they were then, and I trust, always.

Lachlan Ness

Acknowledgements

It is amazing, when one sits down to try to recall all who, wittingly and unwittingly made the writing of this book possible. Names will have been missed. The Book of Acts 9:25 records the lowering of Saul (later Paul, the Apostle) from the wall in Damascus. None of those who risked their lives to aid Saul's escape has been recorded by name, and in the same way, some who, one way and another, helped with this book, won't find their names here. I thank you however from the bottom of my heart.

Again, my wife Janet, our family and friends and those who have enjoyed the previous two books, have all stirred me along when I've slackened off and have needed an encouraging prod.

To the wonderful folk of the Latheron parish who have been warned but who still say they would like to read this book, I offer grateful thanks.

My friends in FAW (Fellowship of Australian Writers Toronto (NSW) branch have been only too ready to suggest minor alterations and have also done some proof-reading.

Our grateful thanks go to our friend, Joanne, for her gracious hospitality during our week in Wishaw, when we stayed with her. During that time she took us to many places we'd never have found without her. We'll never forget her warmth and kindness.

I owe a special debt of gratitude to Sandy and Lyn for their great help and support.

I doubt if the book would have seen the light of day, had it not been for my brother Bill, who is much cleverer than I am and who has great technical and other skills, who prepared the text and cover and probably other things I don't know about, for printing.

Prologue

Kevin, a friend of mine who, like me, is a Presbyterian minister (known around his Australian parish as "Kev the Rev") was keen for a locum position of a few months in Scotland.

One day he told me he was negotiating with a Church of Scotland parish in the north east county of Caithness, the most northerly county on mainland Scotland.

He showed me a paper put out by the Presbytery of Caithness, with details of some vacant parishes.

For some reason, the name of one parish caught my eye: Latheron.

The month was September 2008. My wife Janet and I had been home only a month, after six unforgettable months in the North Isles of Shetland where I had been a locum minister for the Church of Scotland.

I had come home with the thought that the Scottish adventure was over, the thirst to serve there finally satiated. (See "A Kangaroo Loose in Shetland." Lachlan Ness).

In October, a sentence from Kenneth Graham's lovely book, "The Wind in the Willows" popped unannounced into my head:

The Water Rat was restless, and he did not exactly know why. (From the chapter "Wayfarers All").

With something of a shock, I realised that the line applied to me. I was inexplicably disconsolate, a trifle depressed. There was a divine restlessness in me for which I could find no relief.

Looking back now, I think the Lord was leaning on me rather heavily. There was still work to be done.

By then my friend Kevin and his wife Jenny had left for the parish of Thurso, Caithness, and some great adventures in the far north, in a marvellous parish where they were warmly welcomed.

"It would not," I said to myself, "do any harm to contact that vacant parish of Latheron, although they probably have a minister by now," so I did, and they didn't – didn't have a minister, that is. In fact they hadn't had a minister for nine years. I was horrified. A minister had arrived in the North Isles a couple of weeks after I had left, after a vacancy of four years.

It would be marvellous if God blessed the Latheron parish in the same way.

Was there any way I could help?

My prayer went something along the lines of "Lord, if you want me to go, You'll open doors. If You don't, You'll close them."

God did not close doors; in fact He flung them wide open, and the wind of excitement blew in the sweet fragrance of adventure and service in His Name.

Had I said to Janet, "Well, we had a marvellous adventure, but now we can settle down to totter comfortably into our dotage while watching the grandchildren arrive and grow" she would have been delighted. She, however, ever loyal, went along with the new vision.

I know that she, from past experience, has little confidence in my ability to look after myself. She suspected that, left to my own devices, I would probably return in an urn.

Everything fell into place. Even the British High Commission, which had given us such a hard time previously (see "A Kangaroo Loose in Shetland" Lachlan Ness. 2010) was amiable and agreeable. Visas quickly arrived for our stay.

Pauline, the session clerk of the Latheron parish proved helpful and kind, and sent a photo of the beautiful and historic manse, which had been recently refurbished.

A lot of prayer and thought went into the succeeding days, but finally, when it was quite obvious that all paths were clear, we purchased the airline tickets.

Those thoughts were on my mind a week before we left, sitting with a few of our neighbours out under the stars. It was a balmy night, and a February moon rode high, its light filtering softly through the branches of the great old gums.

I knew it would be cold when we arrived in Scotland, but this time, I thought, we'll know how to dress for it. Last time, I took a very warm coat to Shetland, loaned to me by my brother in law. The locals looked at it and commented, "That's a fine summer jacket."

How true were their words! It was great for Australia but not for Shetland. In the icy sub-arctic blasts I may as well have been wearing a singlet.

I smiled when I recalled that, during the day, I had received an email from Ishbel in the North Isles of Shetland, in which she wrote of wild North Sea gales and snow.

It would not be much different in Caithness, in mainland Scotland's far north.

As I looked around our little group that still summer evening, all of us wearing the lightest of summer wear and each holding a cold drink, the incongruity of it hit me. What a difference!

Earlier in the day I had been busy in my study, making final arrangements for our departure. All was arranged, the parish was expecting us and the tickets bought.

I was working under a ceiling fan that was endeavouring to cool the air, while ceiling fans in most rooms of our house "Puddleby on Sea" whirred busily.

The furthest thing from my mind had been ice and snow and North Sea gales…

Chapter 1

The Adventure Begins

A week had passed. We were on our way...

After farewelling our family at Sydney Airport, we had been shown to our seats at the rear of the plane, which was due to take off at 18.05 on Sunday, 15 February 2009. It was not until 18.35 however that our large and crowded aircraft climbed laboriously into a rain-laden sky.

The seat belt light had no sooner gone off than the stout fellow in the seat in front of me put his seat back as far as it could go. If it were not for the protection of the back of the seat, I would have had his head on my lap. He left his seat in that position for the twenty-three hours we were in the air, putting it forward only for meals. To look comfortably at the little TV screen in the seat back, I would have had to have my eyes positioned like a flathead fish's (on the top of my head).

Leaving the seat required the agility of a contortionist . . . a sort of slithering action, accompanied by much grunting and groaning.

Janet, in the aisle seat beside me, was quite comfortable. I slid out of the seat on occasion to stretch the old legs and prevent the dreaded DVT or deep-vein thrombosis.

There was a brief stop at Bangkok, where the pilot nipped out to top up the petrol and do a maintenance check: pull out the dipstick to check the oil, slosh a bit of water into the radiator and give the tyres an experimental kick before ducking off for a quick fag and a cuppa . . . at least, that's the absurd little picture that floated into my tired mind as we shuffled back onto the aircraft after a listless hour or two in the

Bangkok airport lounge, waiting to reboard our aircraft. I supposed it was a fuel stop.

The night dragged on. I peered with sleep-drugged eyes around the darkened tourist class section of the big QANTAS Boeing 747. People were either sleeping or trying to, or peering at their small TV screens. I looked at my screen, which was set on the GPS mode, which told me that we were somewhere over Delhi, about six miles (ten kilometres) below. Looking down through the blackness I could see its lights sprinkled prettily over the dark earth.

Three hours later, we were just about to cross the Caspian Sea. It looked so pleasant on the flight map that I sent word to the pilot that I would like to stop awhile, so that we could enjoy a paddle and a cup of tea. Unfortunately it seems he was one of those drivers who won't stop once he starts, even for a quick toilet break, so we kept going.

We were undergoing the usual twenty-three hours of misery that such journeys generally are from Australia to Britain; at least for us plebs in tourist class.

One hundred years ago, passengers on ships travelled first class, second class and what was known as "steerage." Unfortunate passengers who travelled steerage were put down near the stern of the ship, in cramped cabins (some little more than the size of your average wardrobe), below the waterline, back where the propeller shaft left the ship. Day and night the steerage class passengers were subjected to endless rattling and shaking and noise for at least six weeks on the voyage to Australia.

Down there at the rear of the plane, we were travelling the modern version of steerage. We struck a lot of turbulence, and the tail end of the aircraft responded by endless wagging, shaking and rattling as we struck various patches of rough air.

We slept fitfully. I tried to remember pleasant things to help me sleep.

One memory was recurrent. The previous Friday, I had looked out to our back verandah and was surprised to see a magpie standing on the railing, looking in through the glass sliding door. I knew what he wanted, so rushed in to get some bread. I opened the door, and he walked over casually and took the bread out of my hand. The following morning there was a very loud carolling on the verandah. When I looked, there were TWO magpies there, looking in!

I was utterly charmed to think that I had been summoned by those wild birds that live in the surrounding bush, but are regular visitors to our gentle garden. When pickings are slim, they are not averse to accept a claw-out. (Bird talk for hand-out).

The memory of the beautiful carolling and the sight of those two birds looking in for me, trusting me, cheered me through the long hours of the flight.

As I peered for the hundredth time at the GPS mode of the TV, willing the plane to go faster, I just hoped the GPS in the cockpit was more accurate than one I'd had for my car at one stage.

After its purchase Janet, who'd been chief navigator, found herself demoted to assistant navigator and was resentful. She always referred to the GPS (with a degree of venom usually associated with 'the other woman') as "your toy" with heavy emphasis on "toy" which is why I had nicknamed the GPS Joy – "Joy the Toy."

We'd been on a visit to Canberra and decided to visit the National Museum. Smugly I fed the information into Joy, who led us confidently this way and that until finally she said sweetly, in her posh English accent, "Arriving at destination, on your right."

On the right beside us was an empty brown ploughed paddock.

Janet was beside herself with sinful glee as she heaped scorn upon Joy's electronic and uncaring head. It was quite comical.

Navigating the trackless skies . . . how difficult! My thoughts drifted off to Jim, a farmer and a member of a congregation where I was minister in western New South Wales many years ago. It's a big country out there and many farmers had - probably still have - their own plane, Jim among them. He, like many Australian farmers, had a pleasantly casual approach to life, which unfortunately extended to his small Cessna. Aircraft maintenance was not among Jim's more pressing concerns. If anything broke, it was amazing what he could do with a bit of fencing wire. Instrumentation in the plane was sparse. There was, for instance, no compass; a fact I observed one day while having a look inside. I knew he often went off to sheep and cattle sales at towns many miles away, and sometimes returned at night.

"How do you get about without a compass, Jim?" I asked.

"No worries, Lach," he told me. "In daytime, I simply follow the roads with a map on my knee, but at night, it's different. Before I leave the farm, I capture one of our farm bees and put it in a glass jar. Bees have an infallible homing instinct, so at night I stick the glass jar on the dash and simply fly toward whatever side of the jar the bee is buzzing against. It failed only once, when one dark night I found I'd landed in a neighbour's paddock. I must have picked up one of my neighbour's bees!"

I hoped fervently our pilot's navigation methods were a little more advanced!

Hours later, when people on the eastern side of Australia were possibly thinking thoughts of the evening meal coming up, we were landing at Heathrow, at Terminal 4. It was 6.05am. As we sat there, waiting for permission to leave the aircraft, there was a word from the cockpit: "You will be pleased to learn, folks," the pilot told us cheerfully, "that in the twenty minutes we've been sitting here, the outside temperature has doubled. It is now four degrees."

It took an hour and a half for the interminable processes of customs and security to be finalised. Finally we tottered off, utterly exhausted.

By 8.30am we were soaring into a dull English sky aboard a British Airways A319 Airbus; a much smaller aircraft that seats about 100. After the trip from Australia, it was such a casual journey. For a time I looked upon England's "green and pleasant land" far below: small, hedge-lined fields with remnants of snow piled against them, ponds and streams and gentle hills. It was so lovely. Not too long into the journey however, the clouds rolled in below and all was hidden from view.

An hour later, we landed at Glasgow. After that long journey from Australia, even our excitement was a trifle sluggish, but here we were – Bonnie Scotland at last!

Chapter 2

North to the Highlands

A bus took us to Glasgow station, where we boarded a fast train bound for Inverness – a very comfortable, very quiet and very smooth train.

We sat at a big picture window and watched with interest as the scenery changed on our journey north. The trees on the wooded hills were leafless, reminding us that it was still winter here in the northern hemisphere.

The soft lowland hills disappeared as the terrain became steeper and more rugged. Gently flowing streams gave way to tumbling broad rivers. Great black hills rose around us, holding the last falls of snow in their wintry grasp.

Down in the valleys and glens where the train travelled, forests of fir replaced the leafless birch trees. The stations where we stopped had their names in both English and Gaelic.

There was Stirling, with its famous castle, and Dunblane with its sad history of a mass school shooting. Then there were Glen Eagles and Perth, and Blair Athol. Gaelic names included Baile Chloichridh, which is Pitlochry, and Dail Chuinnidh, or Dalwhinnie, and many others.

We arrived finally at Inbhir Nis (Inverness) at 1.40pm. A friendly taxi driver deposited us at the Thistle Hotel, where we were booked in for the night.

The hotel, situated not far from the railway station, is large and elegant with a lot of parking for vehicles. We were shown to a comfortable room, where a good hot shower and a rest made all the difference.

There is also an office at the hotel for "EuropCars" and it was there that I was told to collect the keys of the car that was to be the Latheron parish car for the next six months.

I made my way to the EuropCars office to collect the keys and look over the car.

The young man in the office took me out to a beautiful little VW Golf diesel manual, silver in colour and almost brand new, with only 170 miles (about 295km) on the clock.

With a cheerful "try not to bend it" he handed me the keys and left me to it.

I was delighted with the choice and took Janet out to have a look. She too was impressed.

The jet lag however was taking its toll, so we tottered up to our room for an early night.

We were both up early, and as our breakfast had cost us £20 (included in the bill of £80) we ate heartily.

We were on the road about 9.30am, heading north. The little Golf was a joy to drive, but the road was unknown and the car unknown so I was a bit wary.

Much as we would have loved a look around Inverness, capital of the Northern Highlands, we were keen to get to our destination.

With some trepidation we set off up the A9, becoming increasingly amazed at the beauty of the country around us.

We crossed the scenic Moray Firth bridge, and then Cromarty Firth bridge.

We had been told of the beauty of the village of Dornoch, and when we saw the sign to it, just after crossing Dornoch firth, I 'chucked a righty' and we went to have a look for ourselves.

The stories are true – it's beautiful, with an aura of timelessness. Take the cars away and one could be walking in streets as they were centuries ago.

We parked in the main street with its lovely old stone houses, and the old stone gaol (inside, it is now a beautiful shop selling very expensive, very classy, clothing and other high quality wares), and went for an amble. There are not many shops, but there is a beautiful 12th century cathedral (where Madonna was married, a lady in a shop told us), which has an attached graveyard dating back to the 6th century AD.

The 12th century bishop personally paid for a castle to be built as his residence, and one of the towers is still original. The rest of the castle has been completely restored to the original and is now a very handsome hotel.

We found a charming little café where we had a cup of coffee. Dornoch is a town well worth a visit or a revisit.

We continued on our merry way north, the traffic getting lighter the further we went. Much of the road runs alongside the North Sea, and some of the views are spectacular.

We passed through many pretty villages and would like to have had time to explore.

I felt rather cheated. In 1998 Janet and I had a six-week holiday in Britain. For part of it we hired a car and made our way north as far as Inverness.

"Don't bother to drive further north," a lady in a travel bureau had told us, "there's only some rocky, uninteresting country between here and John o' Groats, which is Scotland's most northerly point."

None of it had been true, as it turned out, but time was pressing so we'd taken her at her word and headed south. We were now discovering how much we'd been led astray!

Our winding road meandered on, through pretty town and village, usually with the grey North Sea on our right and hills becoming greener and softer the further north we travelled.

This country well to the north of Inverness has been called "the highlands beyond the highlands" for the craggy heights and great mountains further south and west become hills that are lower and gentler and undulating. It is superb grazing land and sheep were everywhere.

About three hours later Janet, who had a road map of Scotland on her lap (the disgraced and humiliated Joy the GPS toy, was back in Australia), said, "We're just about to arrive in Latheronwheel" and sure enough, a minute or two later there it was, its main street off to the right, where we turned.

Latheronwheel is a tiny but picturesque village, with the main street leading down to the little stone harbour. Along its main street, which consisted of one butcher's shop and a few dwellings, we saw a tall, solitary figure and as we approached, he waved.

As we pulled up he came to the car door, smiling a greeting. "Welcome,' he greeted us warmly, "welcome to the parish of Latheron."

It was John, husband of the session clerk, Pauline.

When I got out of the car I realised how tall he was. I came up to about his chest. John was about six and a half feet, and lean with it, with dark curly hair and bright intelligent eyes.

He led us into his cottage, with its views out across green fields. "Pauline's at work," he explained, "but I've a wee bite here for you in the form of a sandwich and a cup of tea, but first you'd best say 'G'day, mate' to Meg." John's attempt at an Australian accent made us laugh. (Do Australians, I asked myself, really say "G'die, mite"?)

He took us to meet her – an utterly adorable, beautiful border collie puppy, only about three months old, her little back end wriggling in time with her tail as she greeted us ecstatically. My love of the border collie/collie breed resurfaced and my thoughts returned to our dear Bonnie, our border collie who had died not long before.

As we ate, John, a full-time deacon of the Church of Scotland who had been filling in at the Latheron parish, told us of his work all over the Presbytery.

He and I discussed what I would be doing over the next few months, and I gained the impression that I was going to be quite busy. He himself was exhausted from his workload. The previous week alone, he told us, he'd had five funerals as well as a memorial service, all around the Presbytery, which was very short of ministers and deacons and so every parish called on his services.

Later, we followed John in his car to the village of Lybster, about five miles further north. On the way we passed through the village of Latheron, where the A9 turns off to the north-west, while we kept heading north, joining the A99, following the coast.

Finally, we were there: Lybster. Just opposite a fine looking hotel called "The Portland Arms" was the turn-off down to the main street. We could see a long line of grey houses. A few hundred metres down, John stopped outside a big grey church with a fine house beside it.

We joined him on the footpath. "Here," said John, pointing, "is the Lybster Church, and there beside it is the manse."

We recognised both from the photos that Pauline had sent us. The manse was a handsome, double-storey building with dormer windows, set well off the road and listed by the Scottish National Trust.

We looked at it admiringly. "It's lovely, John," I said.

John led us down the path, opened the door and invited us in with a smile and a flourish.

The congregation had had the manse completely refurbished, and had done it superbly. All the furniture we would need had been added, all tastefully chosen. As well, Janet found crockery and cutlery, and there were some lovely personal touches, such as a vase of fresh flowers, a welcome card and some delightful little ornaments. Food had been placed in the refrigerator.

John and Pauline had put in a spare TV of theirs. Everything has been so thoughtfully and lovingly done for us and we felt most honoured. The manse was indeed a beautiful home.

The study had a fine desk and some bookshelves. From its window I looked out across green fields to a farmhouse. On the desk someone had placed a teddy bear, wearing a little tartan bow tie, its arms wide in welcome. I was quite moved by that thoughtful touch.

Later, after John left, we went for a walk down the village street. A sense of exhilaration and excitement flooded through me. We were here at last! This village would be our home town for the next six months!

Lybster is an old village, with four small shops. One was a newsagency, which included the post office, another a butcher's shop, another a small general store and the other also a wonderfully old fashioned, small general store. We opened the door and the doorbell tinkled a welcome, just as shops did when I was a boy. Inside, there was practically everything one's heart could desire in the grocery line, and on the walls there were a couple of shelves holding old-fashioned jars, containing a wide variety of lollies.

At the sound of the bell a man hurried in from another room; a smallish man about my age, grey haired and with a warm smile. I could see he had just finished eating.

I smiled back. "Sorry to interrupt your meal," I said.

He looked at us more closely. "Hullo – that accent! You must be our new minister! I'm Eric – Welcome! Eileen, come and meet the Australian minister and his wife!"

A lady, small and motherly and very welcoming, hurried in. "Come in! Come in! We live at the back of the shop. Come in for a cup of tea!"

She took us through to her warm and cosy kitchen and parlour, as Eric hurried off to the sound of the shop bell.

"You've come to the right place," she told us over tea and some delicious home-made shortbread, "we're members of the Kirk and I'm an elder. Now if there's anything you need, we're just a wee bit down the street, so don't forget to call us."

On our wandering a few people in the village greeted us. "Are you the new locum minister? Welcome to our village!"

Back at the manse, the doorbell rang. It was Eileen, Eric's cheerful wife, with more home cooking for us, including a large pot of delicious-smelling soup.

I had a feeling that we were going to be spoiled...

Chapter 3

Add-on John

We spent the next day doing some exploring around Lybster, and found our way down to the pretty walled harbour, with its small white lighthouse. A number of small commercial fishing boats were tied to the quay. It was a scene that delighted us.

During the afternoon, John rang. "Pauline and I would like to take you both to dinner this evening, Lach," he told me. "Meet us over at the Portland Arms about 6.30."

We were there a little early, for the hotel was only a short walk from the manse.

I waited with interest to see Pauline, for after seeing tall John, I had a mental picture of an unusually tall lady. I was in for a shock. Accompanying John was a small, petite, fair-haired and attractive lady, seemingly half John's height.

Her eyes lit up when she saw us. "It's so marvellous to have you here at last!" she said as she greeted us with a hug.

It was a delightful meal. They both worked extremely hard for their Church. Pauline held a senior executive position with the NHS and as well was a highly qualified registered nurse, who still taught midwifery from time to time.

It was sad, listening to the story of that small country parish that had been without a minister for nine years. The congregation had spent a great deal of money, refurbishing the manse, hoping to interest a suitable minister.

Pauline and John proved very easy to talk to and in no time we were conversing like old friends.

"Pauline," I told her earnestly, "you're the best-looking session clerk I've ever worked with, or am likely to work with, now that I've retired from full-time ministry."

"I presume your former session clerks were all male?" Pauline asked sweetly.

"Um – well, yes."

She smiled and shook her head. "I've heard all about you Australians and your tall tales!"

We took the opportunity to discuss strategies to attract a minister. Refurbishing the manse was one idea. For a vacant parish there are various ways to make the vacancy known across the country and even abroad. We would explore all those avenues and of course, as John pointed out, there is the priceless value of the prayers of faithful people.

Just as we were making preparations to leave a voice called "Hullo, John."

We looked up. Standing beside the table was a short, stout, middle-aged man in a dark, slightly grubby-looking overcoat. He had bright blue eyes and was smiling engagingly at John. I thought he looked a very pleasant man. He nodded politely to Pauline and us.

John's voice, I thought, carried something less than enthusiasm: "Oh. Hullo, Addon."

There was an awkward pause. Finally John nodded to us. "This is our locum minister and his wife, Rev Lachlan and Mrs Ness."

The man John called Addon regarded us with bright and interested eyes and proffered his hand. "Very pleased to meet you, Mr and Mrs Ness. It's a pleasure to meet you. If there is any way I can help you, please let me know. I'll do anything I can to make your stay here in our village as happy as possible" I was quite charmed by his warm greeting and equally puzzled by John's attitude.

After he'd gone, John warned, "Be careful if you have any dealings with that man. Don't be fooled by his 'hail fellow well-met' approach. In fact count your fingers after you've shaken hands. He lives in Wick where he runs a run-down backpackers' place at exorbitant rates for unwary backpackers, among other things, but he has a small flat here in Lybster where he spends a fair bit of his time. He also runs some sort of an illegal taxi service I think."

"That's amazing, John! He seemed so genuine!"

The deacon laughed. "That's his stock in trade of course. It's fooled many – for a while."

I was puzzled. "Addon... that's a strange name. Is it German or something?"

John smiled. "No. His name is John, but in all his business dealings, just when people think it's all cut and dried and they're ready to pay, he'll say 'Oh – I forgot to add on the cost of...' whatever he can think up. Over the years he's come to be known as 'Add-on John' which in time was shortened simply to 'Addon.' He's had the nickname for so long now that most people can't remember his real name."

Next day we drove 20km or so along the winding A99, with the North Sea to the right, through some small villages into the town of Wick, similar in many ways to Lerwick, capital of Shetland, with its ancient stone buildings and picturesque, narrow winding streets. We found it quite fascinating.

Wick is the major town on the east side of Caithness where folk go to do their main shopping. On the northern outskirts is a huge Tesco store, and it was there that Janet was aiming for.

"While we're here, Janet," I said, "I'll have to get a box of blank DVDs as back-up for the stuff on the lap-top computer," so in the store we parted.

On my mind was a disastrous computer crash a year previously, when I'd lost a year of hard work. To have it happen now would be the ultimate disaster.

I made my way down to the large electrical section. I found what I wanted – the last box, and with a sigh of relief, picked it up.

Just as I did so I was startled by a voice behind me: "Hullo, Mr Ness! Found what you're looking for?"

I turned, to find myself face to face with none other than the dodgy one known as Add-on John, and the deacon's warning came flooding back.

"Yes," I said shortly but not wanting to appear rude; "I'm after this box of blank DVDs, to back up some stuff on my computer."

He looked at the box. "Looks like you got the last one too. By coincidence, Mr Ness, I have this exact article in my warehouse that I can let you have for about half this price, and – no, no! They are not

stolen or hot anything like that. I got them at a closing down sale."
Addon had looked up and I suspected had seen my wary look.

I paused. We'd been spending money like drunken sailors since
leaving home. My first stipend payment was still a month away and I
knew Janet's shopping trolley with goods to stock the manse would be
full to overflowing.

"Half this price... Are you certain that's what the cost will be?"

"Of course!"

"I can return any damaged ones and be reimbursed?"

"Naturally."

"I need them immediately. When can I get them?"

"I'll deliver them personally this afternoon."

It seemed a straightforward deal. I could not see how I could
possibly lose.

I put the lone box back on the shelf. "OK then. I'll see you this
afternoon."

When I found Janet she told me she'd spent over £80.00, doing a
very large shop, stocking up the fridge and freezer, as well as buying
fruit and vegetables and other necessary items. "Mony a mickle makes a
muckle!" my old Scottish Granny had always been at pains to teach me.
It means "all the little bits make a big bit." She was referring to money,
and we needed to save 'mony a mickle' just now.

I did not mention my deal with Addon to Janet. She has a very black
and white approach to those sorts of things. John had told us to have
nothing to do with Addon; therefore don't. Simple as that. I am more
gullible, and as a result have suffered for my folly numerous times over
the years. Sadly, the experiences don't seem to teach me. I seem to be a
slow learner in questions of trust.

On the way back we went to the hospital, where I made my first
pastoral visit although officially I wasn't due to start until 1st March.

Wick hospital is the major hospital in the County and is very
impressive. It's where Pauline worked.

John had told me that George, a staunch member of the congregation
and an elder, had had a stroke, but was bright and cheerful and has been
left with no speech or other impairment.

I found him in one of the wards and introduced myself to a cheerful,
elderly man who did not appear too concerned about his complaint.

"Ye ken it's no' mah furrst stroke," he informed me with a smile. "Ah'm used tae them!"

George was a mine of information. As we chatted he suddenly asked, "Have you heard of the Whalegoe steps?" I hadn't.

"There's a small harbour between here and Lybster which is at the bottom of a sheer cliff. To get to it, the fishermen cut steps down the side of the cliff – three hundred and sixty-five of them, one for every day of the year. Near the bottom there's a broad clearing where the fishermen built a shed and a smoke-house to dry the fish. To put their boats in the water they had to winch them doon another twenty feet or so.

"Periodically, schooners would arrive and were backed in - no motors, you mind – all done by brilliant seamanship. The barrels of herring were loaded aboard and transported all over Europe. Some of the catch of course was sold locally. The women came down wi' baskets that fitted on their backs, and they carried the loaded baskets all the way back up the three hundred and sixty-five steps. When I'm well again, I'd like to take you and your wife down those steps. Back at the top, you'll be completely puffed. Imagine what it was like for the womenfolk, with a great basket of herring on their backs!"

George also told me that he lives not far from the biggest peat bog in the world.

"A few years ago, a body was discovered there in the bog," he said. "When it was brought to the surface it was noted that the clothing was from the Jacobean period, so the body had been there for centuries. Poor wretch was possibly murdered, or perhaps he just wandered off and fell in. The corpse looked as fresh as the day the luckless fellow disappeared, but in the fresh air it quickly disintegrated."

George mentioned ancient burial cairns and brochs (stone-age forts) around the district; some older than the pyramids, that are well worth exploring.

On the way back to Lybster, looking out to sea, we could see two North Sea oil rigs in plain view, a few miles out.

At 2.00pm, there was a knock on the door. I raced to get there before Janet and when I did so, there was Addon, smiling cheerfully, holding a box of DVDs identical to the one at Tesco.

I carefully closed the door. "Thank you, Addon! That was..." I pulled out my wallet.

Addon jumped in. He named a price exactly double the Tesco price.

I couldn't believe my ears. "WHAT??"

"You told me you needed them at once, Mr Ness," said Addon apologetically, "so I decided to deliver them personally. I've had to add on the cost of freight, you see. I brought them all the way from Wick for you."

I suspected that was a lie. He had a dwelling in Lybster. I also knew that if I lost the data sitting in my computer I'd be put back weeks in preparation. I knew too that to refuse to buy Addon's would mean a trip to Wick and back, to a shelf that by now could be bare. Addon had me and I think he knew it. He held out the box, still smiling cheerfully. Suddenly it occurred to me that this was possibly the very same box I'd picked up and put back in Wick. Addon probably ducked back and picked it up after I'd left. I felt my face go red with frustrated anger.

I grabbed the box, shoved the money angrily at him and shut the door hard, ignoring his "Thank you Mr -"

I stamped into the study and threw the box onto the desk. I was so annoyed I was shaking, and knew I'd have to wait before I did anything potentially delicate on the computer.

"Who was that, dear?" Janet called from the kitchen.

"No one worth worrying about" I replied, which was true enough.

Later in the afternoon we went back to Pauline's and John's house at Latheronwheel, to meet the elders of the parish, who were keen to meet us. On the dining room table there was a banquet that would have fed an army.

There were about a dozen elders there, male and female, with spouses (a couple could not make it) who greeted us most warmly, and were fascinated to learn something of Australia. They had been following the bushfire stories with horror.

I was looking forward to Sunday for I still had a week after that before I started officially, so Janet and I could be pew sitters.

"A lady, Heather Stewart, will be preaching on Sunday," Pauline had told me; "who is what is known in the Church of Scotland as a lay reader. They do a preaching course. She's an excellent preacher and lives in Wick."

On Sunday we made our way next door, into the Church. Big and square on the outside, made of solid grey stone, like many of the buildings in the village, the Church was very attractive inside, with lots of warm wood and a large, high and handsome centre pulpit that had a beautiful stained glass window above it.

We stood at the door and were introduced to the congregation by Pauline as they arrived. Young and old alike greeted us warmly, and I began to look forward to meeting them all in their own homes.

Heather the preacher was small, bright-eyed and I guessed about forty or so. I'd been told she was a teacher. She was also a happy extrovert. Half way through the first hymn she held up her hand. "Stop!" she called. We stopped.

"Why are you singing in that lack-lustre fashion? You're supposed to be praising God! Put some life into it!" We put some life into it.

Heather's service was great. She had a very good children's address and lived up to Pauline's assessment of her as a first-rate preacher. Those who think women don't have a pulpit ministry gift should listen to her and others like her.

Now, I thought, they are going to get me, and I fear that may be a disappointment, if what I heard today is anything to go by. Oh well, I thought, all I can do is do my best, be myself and leave the rest to God...

We had not long had lunch when the doorbell rang. It was Lorraine, another of the elders, a cheerful lady who had the broadest of Caithness accents. Lorraine was a systems analyst.

"Hullo – hope I'm not interfering" she said cheerfully as we welcomed her in; "I thought I'd get your Internet working for you."

The congregation had connected the Internet to the manse but I had no idea how to get it connected to the laptop computer I'd brought from Australia.

Lorraine had it all up and running in about five minutes. Now we could communicate easily with family and friends.

That evening Janet and I went to a little service, held monthly, in the Lybster Day Care Centre. It was informal, excellently run by John the Deacon and was followed by supper. The elderly folk who found it hard to get to the normal service and sit in the hard pews really appreciated it, and they told me so.

"From now on, you'll be conducting this one too, Lachlan," John said, grinning; "I'm retiring!" It was a very cold night. Snow was forecast for the coming week, John told us.

A day or so later I had a chat with the local constable. The police station was exactly opposite the manse and had a residence attached. His name was Keith; a tall, dark-haired man with keen eyes and a weathered complexion. He lived in the police house with his wife and a couple of young children. I introduced myself as a part time NSW police chaplain. He was interested to see my badge. In our chat I mentioned briefly my dealing with Addon John.

When I told him how Addon had 'done me like a dinner,' Keith laughed.

"I'm sorry to laugh, Lach, but it's so like the man! He operates just inside the law. We thought we had him once, when he stepped too far over the line. When we went in for him he was given the usual caution: you know, 'You are not obliged to say anything but anything you do say may be taken down and used in evidence against you…' etc. Well, when he heard that, he laughed. 'Thanks for the tip!" he said; "I'll no' be telling you anything in that case!' The trouble was, our whole case rested on his confession. He wouldn't open his mouth, so despite our other evidence, we had to let him go." What a pity, I thought.

Chapter 4

Finding our feet

It was nearing the end of February – the end of summer in Australia, nearly the end of winter in Scotland, where spring starts on 20th March. The sudden shock to the system, a rapid transfer from the heat of an Australian late summer to the chill of a northern Scottish late winter, certainly had an effect on us. We soon discovered the value of gloves, beanies, thermals and thick socks. We were also told that there is no such thing as cold weather in Scotland – only inadequate clothing!

On the positive side, we were charmed by the beauty of the area in which found ourselves and also by the friendliness of everyone with whom we came into contact.

The village of Lybster is not large, and so most folk seemed to be aware of the arrival of the minister and his wife from the antipodes.

"Oh – so you're the new minister from Australia?" a lady said to me; "I heard about you in the butcher's shop."

I was also asked to write a little personal profile about us in the village paper called "The Back Street Bletherer" which was run by another Lorraine, who was very committed to her paper.

I still recall my dear old Scots granny saying crossly to us boys: "Stop that blathering noo!" when we were noisily talking or arguing.

"The Bletherer" was highly popular as a source of local news and just about everyone bought a copy each fortnight.

We spent a few days finding our feet in the figurative sense. Sometimes they were so frozen it was hard to find them in the actual sense.

We bought a television licence, which one has to do over here, which is horribly expensive: £139.00. (About $AUD 300.00).

We went to Wick one day to join the local library and were fascinated to note that the library cards we were given are in both English and Gaelic.

I'd already been out to visit Pat, the very competent Lybster organist who lived with her husband Lawrence on a farm a few miles from the village. Her small, lithe fingers could work wonders on the church organ. On one visit she invited me to come along to the choir practice. "Actually," she told me, "it's not a choir at all. We call ourselves JABOS."

"That's an unusual name," I commented.

Pat smiled. "It is, rather. We don't believe we're good enough to be called a choir so we call ourselves 'just a bunch of singers' – hence JABOS." I had to laugh – but listening to them that night at the practice, I thought they were very good.

Shortly after our arrival we had an unusual visitor. He was Jim Morrison, the only other minister in the Latheron parish, who belonged to the Free Presbyterian Church of Scotland. He was a big man with warm eyes that matched his personality.

We were immediately taken by his genuine warmth and kindness. Here was a man who would be a good friend, and so he turned out to be. Jim was a Caithness man, born and bred, from Thurso, the other big town in the county of Caithnes, and about the same size as Wick.

"You'll have to come to our manse and have a meal with us. I'd like you to meet my wife Cathy," he told us.

On our second week I went off with John the deacon to the Dunbeath junior school to conduct religious education.

"You and Jim Morrison will be sharing the religious education," John told me, "month about. This coming month it's your turn."

Dunbeath is fourteen kilometres south of Lybster; a small village of two shops. Old-world beautiful, most of its buildings are classified by the Scottish National Trust, and was the place where I would conduct the service of worship in the Dunbeath Church each Sunday at 10.00am.

On my first visit to the school I wore a jacket with an Australian flag on the pocket. The school was small, with about a dozen children or so, up to age twelve. The principal, Alan, made me welcome and introduced me to his staff of one teacher, a teacher's aid and a secretary, before leading John and me in to meet the children.

John conducted the class in his easy, genial way and soon had the children eating out of his hand, for he knew them all. They were eager to learn about Australia, and knew all about kangaroos and koalas and possums but were a bit vague when it came to wombats and numbats and other lesser-known Australian natives.

I had a most entertaining time with the children and afterwards we enjoyed morning tea in the staff room.

When we left the school, John asked, "Have you ever heard of Dunbeath castle?"

I told him I hadn't. "Let's go then," he said, so we did.

We drove a short distance from the school to a road with a sign that read "Private Road" which John ignored. We were now in the grounds of Dunbeath castle.

Some distance down, we turned into an avenue of beautiful trees, with woods either side, still bare, but the ground around the trees was white with pretty flowers called snowdrops.

Ahead, I saw it, and my eyes opened wide – a beautiful castle with handsome turrets, looking as if it were a painting straight out of a picture book, while from the high mast on the battlements, Scotland's flag, the St Andrew's cross, flew proudly.

I could hardly believe my eyes. The castle was beautiful beyond description, standing on the edge of a cliff, overlooking the North Sea.

"Is it a museum?" I wanted to know.

"Och, that is no museum," John assured me; "it's a family home."

I am not sure how many acres the property stood on, but it was a lot. John took me to another part of the property, where a great stone wall stood, about three metres high, surrounded a beautiful garden of many acres, attended by gardeners.

We entered by a wooden door in the wall and saw some gardeners working busily.

No one seemed surprised to see us, and they all seemed to know John. The high, walled garden is a picture of old world charm, with a long greenhouse, trees and hedges, flowers, a large vegetable patch and an ornamental fountain, all lovingly attended by the gardening staff.

As we walked back to the car a smart four-wheeled trap, pulled by a white horse, came trotting around a bend, with a solitary lady holding the reins.

"That lady and her husband own the castle," John informed me.

John waved, and the lady drew the horse to a halt. She was tall and elegant, and gave us a welcoming smile.

"Good morning!" John called, and it was obvious he knew her. "I'd like you to meet our locum minister who will be in the Latheron parish for the next six months".

We introduced ourselves. She was a most pleasant lady and chatted to us for a while before giving the reins a flick and departing.

As we drove off, John said, "Have you seen Dunbeath harbour yet?"

I hadn't, so my guide decided it would be a good time to go. We drove the short distance, down past a picturesque old stone bridge across a bubbling burn to a small and very pretty harbour, which, like all the harbours along this section of the coast, I'd been told, had been built for the herring trade.

Tied to the breakwater was a handsome red fishing boat, its stern loaded with lobster pots. The motor was chugging away and it was obvious the vessel was about to put to sea. A man in yellow overalls was assisting the departure.

John said "That's Bob's' son's boat, and that's Bob helping. It should be OK if we go down. I don't think they're superstitious."

I looked at him. "Superstitious? What do you mean?"

John grinned. "There was a time around these parts, if fishermen were walking to their boats to leave for the fishing, and met a minister, or a nun or a priest, they'd turn around and go home. The old superstition is not entirely gone among some."

"You're kidding!"

"I assure you, I kid you not," John replied, "but they're not all like that."

I was a trifle miffed to learn that my arrival on the scene would be regarded as an ill omen.

By the time we had walked to the breakwater, the little red fishing boat had moved off and was heading out into the troubled dark waters of the North Sea.

We chatted to Bob for a time; an elderly man whose back prevented him from going to sea after a lifetime as a fisherman. Now he was free to help his son.

Not far from the harbour I saw a small statue. It looked like a young boy, struggling to carry a huge fish.

"What's that, John?" I asked.

"Many years ago" the deacon explained, "a famous author lived here called Neil Gunn. He wrote many books of life around this part of Scotland, and one book was called Highland River. The statue is of Kenn and the Salmon, characters in the book, and the statue was erected in memory of Neil Gunn."

Back at the manse, I related to Janet all that had transpired during the morning.

"Why wasn't I there to see the castle?" wailed my wife when I told her of the morning's adventures; "I suppose I'll never see it now!"

Of course that is simply the way the wily female mind works. Naturally I responded by offering to take her that very afternoon.

In the grounds of Dunbeath castle we drove down the long avenue of trees towards the castle itself. I felt very uncomfortable as we pulled up near the castle door. Those people did not know us. The sign at the entrance said it all: "Private Road." I felt a trespasser – we were trespassers.

Janet stared, amazed, at the sight of the magnificent castle. "It's like something out of a fairy story!" she exclaimed.

"OK," I said, "we've seen it. Let's go."

I was just about to drive off when I was dismayed to see the door open and someone emerge – probably to give us our marching orders in a politely icy way, I thought.

It was the lady of the household; the one I had met earlier with John.

She came to the car door and I introduced Janet.

She smiled a welcome. "Would you like to look around?" she offered.

We jumped at the chance, and were shown the grounds immediately around the castle, built out on its headland. It would have been devilishly tricky for an enemy to attack. The view from the rear of the castle was breathtaking.

Our guide explained that the front of the castle was genuine 12th or 13th century, while the rear was designed by a famous 19th century architect.

As we got back to the car she asked "Would you like to see inside?"

Would we ever! Our gracious hostess led us in, where we were greeted by her two lovely dogs. Inside, the castle was much as I imagined, only better, with its great majestic rooms, high ceilings and beautiful staircase. The views up and down the coast from the great windows were even more breathtaking.

Despite its size, the interior of the castle had a quiet, homely feel about it, for the furnishings were superb and selected with impeccable taste.

Finally we farewelled that charming and hospitable lady, whose parting word was to invite us to look around the garden on the way out. Having been there, it was a pleasure to show Janet around the walled garden and she, being a gardener to her fingertips, appreciated it more than I ever could.

We left, grateful for, and a little overwhelmed by, the kindly welcome that had been accorded us at Dunbeath castle.

Chapter 5

John o' Groats

We dearly wanted to familiarise ourselves with our district, so one day we drove to the village of John o' Groats, about fifty kilometres to the north, the most northerly town on mainland Scotland. It's a pretty drive, and the country reminded us so much of beautiful Shetland, with its soft rolling hills, rugged coastline and absence of trees.

When we arrived, a boisterous wind was blowing straight off the North Sea, and it was freezing!

John o' Groats is tiny and sits on the north-eastern tip of the Scottish mainland. It has a few touristy shops, a garage and post office. Each year, hundreds come up from Land's End, the most southerly tip of England by all sorts of means: by walking, cycling, motorcycling, driving. One year a fellow arrived on a penny-farthing bicycle. "Land's End to John o' Groats" is a goal many set themselves in the summer, travelling from mainland Britain's most southerly point to its most northerly point.

A large and unusual-looking house sits not far from the shore, which was the home of the Dutchman Jan De Groot, who came to be known as John o' Groats. He built the house with eight-bedrooms and eight doors all opening to the outside, for his eight children.

At the tiny harbour we looked out to the grey tossing waters of the North Sea where we could see a ferry, making its way across the dangerous waters of Pentland Firth. Beyond lay the small, uninhabited island of Stroma, the houses of its former occupants still plainly visible.

Beyond Stroma we could just make out the most southerly islands of the Orkneys.

We popped in to the little tourist shop by the jetty and bought a few odds and ends before making our way across the road for lunch. Attached to the café is a shopper's delight – a store selling all sorts of beautiful Scottish woollens and other wares.

We had lunch and then Janet insisted on exploring the woollen wares.

Sadly, I must confess that I, and not she, succumbed and spent up. The object of my desire was a Harris Tweed sports jacket. I've had a few over the years. The tweed is produced on the island of Harris on the west coast of Scotland. It is beautiful material and never wears out. Over the years I have "outgrown" one or two.

The trouble was, there was a sale of Harris Tweed jackets, reduced from £140.00 to £90.00. That is far cheaper than one can purchase a Harris Tweed jacket in Australia. I couldn't resist the temptation – I bought one.

Already we didn't know how we were going to put in the extras into our suitcases when we returned to Australia, without going over the twenty kilo each limit.

Soon after arriving in Lybster I became quickly addicted to the jelly beans that Eric and Eileen sold in their shop; huge, colourful monsters, the like of which I'd never seen before, and haven't since.

My addiction did not please Janet, who is always mindful of health issues including weight gains and inconvenient complications such as diabetes, so I generally made sure I was alone when I purchased the beans, and had sworn Eric and Eileen to secrecy – not, of course, that Janet was fooled. In her nursing career she dealt with people far cagier than I.

A day after our trip to John o' Groats, I made my furtive way into the shop and put in an order for "the usual" – a quarter pound bag of my addiction. Eric always weighed them carefully, as a good businessman should, before placing them in the bag, but Eileen, among the kindliest and most generous people I have ever met, often slipped in one or two extra, or handed one or two across the counter, with a conspiratorial smile.

"Lachlan," Eileen said to me as she handed me a couple of extra beans; "did you happen to notice a crippled lady in Church on Sunday?

She was sitting near the back." As a matter of fact I had. She was tallish, elegant and had a 'presence.' She was hard not to notice.

"She's our Ladies' Guild president," Eileen explained, "and has been for some time. She was a high school teacher and taught at Wick. She rules us with a rod of iron, but in the gentlest possible way. It's sad, the way she was crippled. As a child she caught some hideous disease that nearly killed her, but when she recovered, she was crippled. It never stopped her from doing just about anything, including playing golf. She was born here, you know. Her father had a farm. She never married. Margaret is very quiet about it, but I can tell you she has cancer now. No one knows what's going to happen, but her time could be short. You'll love going to see her – she has six cats."

I'd have gone to see Margaret anyway, but my ears pricked up at that. Not many people I'd met so far in the parish had cats, at least house cats, and as a cat lover I felt deprived. I needed a 'cat fix.' I still mourned the death of Singh, our beautiful Burmese, back in Australia, some time before.

I am quite comfortable with being a cat lover and know I am in some excellent company, including that of the great American author Mark Twain, who once wrote that heaven would not be heaven for him, unless his cats were there with him. I've always felt the same, much as I love dogs.

Later that day I went to see Margaret at her little home in the village, taking Janet with me. When we knocked on the door she called us in.

She was seated in the parlour by an electric fire that blazed cheerily in the hearth, for it was a chilly day. Books and newspapers were everywhere, and on every comfortable chair, a cat was sleeping, apparently unconcerned at the intrusion. It was the pleasantest of scenes and exuded an atmosphere of contentment, calm and peace.

Margaret's eyes lit up with pleasure when she saw us, for our visit was unannounced.

"Come in, come in!" she greeted us; "it's so lovely to see you! Find a chair and I'll make us a cup of tea."

She struggled to her feet and made her way towards the kitchen, holding on to the wall for support. I went to help, but Janet laid a restraining hand on my arm.

"I think Margaret wants to be completely independent," she whispered.

We'd each found a seat by the time she returned with the tea. By that time I had a large black and white cat on my knee and could feel the rumble of his purr under my hand.

Margaret smiled. "That's Red. He's the oldest here. When you put him down, do it carefully, for he's nearly blind."

It seemed an odd name for a black and white cat but Margaret told us that was the name he had when he arrived, abandoned by a family nearby that had moved on.

On the chair beside me, regarding me with bright, impassive green eyes was a small cat with tabby markings, part-Persian. I put out my hand to her, but she jumped off the chair and wandered out of the room.

"Och, that's Tilly," said Margaret. "She's the flichter."

The 'ch' in the word was pronounced using the soft guttural that Scots use but which many Australians find very difficult, usually pronouncing it as a hard 'k', such as 'lock' instead of 'loch.' I, happily, have no trouble with the guttural, but it's beyond Janet.

"What's a flichter," Margaret?" I asked.

"Flichter means 'flighty'" Margaret explained; "It's a Caithness word."

We were to learn later that Margaret was considered an authority on the Caithness dialect and unique Caithness words, and had written extensively on the subject.

Being in Margaret's company was to feel rested, and that's the way we felt when we got back to the manse.

Later that night as I sat in the study, a gale was blowing outside. I could hear its moaning through the thick stone walls of the great house with its double glazed windows. I could see the icy rain slashing at the windows.

My thoughts were with Bob's son, the fisherman. If he is out there on the great waters, I thought, I hope sight of me wasn't on his mind, but rather thoughts of Him who rules both the wind and the waves.

Chapter 6

"Getting to Know You…"

I thought that my first day of preaching would have been on Sunday, 1ˢᵗ March, but it was not to be. I had learned that news the previous week, when I was told that the Latheron parish's Worship Group would be conducting. I was delighted, and on the Thursday evening had gone out to Andrew's and Jean's fine home, with its marvellous views out across green fields to the North Sea, where the Worship Group met regularly. It was the Worship Group, together with John the deacon, which made sure the pulpit was filled each Sunday.

When I'd first met Andrew and Jean, it seemed to me that Andrew might have had some antipathy towards Australians, but very soon realised that here was a man of great faith and also a man with a great sense of humour, and his cracks about Australians were very funny, and meant to be no more than that. Anyway, Australians are very good at dishing it out, so have to be prepared to take it. Soon he and I, Janet and Jean, were very good friends. Andrew taught at the local school

The Worship Group usually officiated at least once each month, and the following Sunday was to be its turn.

There was no doubt in my mind that the parish was still strong and reasonably vibrant because of John and the Worship Group. After a nine-year vacancy, many a parish would have had almost no members. People are inclined to wander off to find spiritual nourishment elsewhere when there is no regular ministry.

The worship group comprised six or so. We gathered in the big, comfortable lounge room with its glowing log fire and were joined by Watson, a whippet, the family dog, who greeted everyone affectionately. It was not a long meeting and commenced with supper to get us going. We discussed hymns and readings, and John the deacon was given the job of preaching the sermon. I relaxed, sat back and listened, knowing I was going to be a pew sitter again, but ready and willing to help if needed.

It was a close-knit group and I was being made to feel part of it. I felt quite honoured, and appreciated the warm friendship being extended.

The Sunday Service was a great success. It was a combined service, for the folk from the Dunbeath Church came up for it, so we had a chance to meet them too. John preached remarkably well and the JABOS singers sang like angels, as I told them later. They were all highly amused but I hope pleased.

During the service, Janet and I were introduced and asked to say something about ourselves. The service was followed by morning tea, so we had chance to start putting names to faces.

I think we all left feeling as Janet and I did – uplifted.

When I awoke the next day it was to find Janet already up and about, and I could hear the sound of voices speaking in Gaelic. She had found the Gaelic programme on radio Scotland. Occasionally she put it on for a listen and the music was always lovely.

I had just dressed when Janet walked into the bedroom. "There's no heating in the house," she announced.

That was the start of a great deal of activity. I was horrified at the thought that we may have gone through the 1,000 litres of heating oil that had been delivered to the manse on the day of our arrival. How could we possibly go through 1,000 litres in three weeks? Investigation however revealed that the flame had gone out.

About 9.00am a ferociously wild gale blew in from the west, bringing with it freezing rain. At 12.00 the oil heating light went out again, so again I went out in the wild wind and driving rain, getting it going once more. It happened later in the day but that was the end of it.

It was too wild to do anything at all outside, so we concentrated on work inside.

The following day Janet and I applied for a Scottish bus pass for each of us, which would provide free bus travel all over Scotland. We were eligible because we were retired, had a TV licence and a Scottish address, and I would be paying tax.

Chapter 7

'I lift my eyes...'

"How do I look?" I asked Janet nervously. It was the Sunday when I was to preach at both Dunbeath and Lybster for the first time. We were standing in the vestry of the pretty Dunbeath Church, known as the Dunbeath Ross Church. I had on dark suit, clerical collar, preaching gown, preaching bands, preaching scarf; the traditional garb of traditional ministers of the Presbyterian Church. Janet had come into the vestry with me to give me some last minute encouragement. I'd always been afflicted by some initial stage-fright, even then, thirty-nine years since ordination.

"You look fine, dear," Janet assured me; "just be your normal self, and relax."

She left and Ken arrived to escort me into the service.

I'd been to see Judy, the Dunbeath organist, who told me she was keen on the Scottish metrical Psalms (as I am), so I decided we'd start each Service at Dunbeath by singing one of the great old metrical Psalms. The parish was blessed in having two excellent organists in Judy and Pat.

It was quite a lovely service, made all the more so by the warm acceptance of the folk of the Dunbeath Church.

We'd bordered on being late for the service. It was a bright and sunny if cold morning. On the way down from Lybster we'd been swept up in the beauty of Morven, the highest hill in Caithness, glistening brightly in the sun, completely covered in snow, like the finest white icing, its grandeur dominating all. We stopped the car to take numerous photos. Next to Morven, smaller hills swept away into the distance, all covered in snow. "The smaller hill beside Morven is called 'the pap'" Judy the organist told me.

I looked. She did not have to explain why. "The name of Morven is from the Gaelic," Judy continued, "which is A' Mhor Bheinn, which in English means 'to live by the sea' and Morven is certainly not far from the sea."

Half an hour after the Benediction at Dunbeath Church I was ready to start the service at Lybster Church. One of the elders was with me in the vestry. "Here's the wireless microphone,' he said, handing it to me with a smile. "It's off now, but don't forget to turn it on when you go to the pulpit. Don't forget to turn it off afterwards either. We once had a minister who turned it on just before the service was due to start, then decided to go to the toilet first but forgot tae turn it off. It was not an elevating experience for the congregation, I can tell you!"

Again, I was relieved and pleased when the service went well. The Jabos group sang a great little anthem, Pat played the organ beautifully and I made no glaring errors; something not unknown when I am a little nervous.

Chapter 8

A tale of two crooks

On Tuesday I set off for my first class of religious instruction at the Dunbeath school. It was a freezing morning, and on the way down it started to sleet, then snow.

The children were delightful country kids and not hard to control, but there was a teacher in the room anyway. Again, they wanted to know all about Australia.

The headmaster and his staff made me welcome in the staff room afterwards over morning tea, and joining them after the religious instruction class became a very pleasant routine.

On the way back to Lybster I decided to call in on John and Bella, elderly members of the Dunbeath congregation. John was a retired shepherd but had a small croft, and even in his old age worked with the agility and strength of a man half his years.

John had a fascinating little hobby, making shepherds' crooks. He showed me a couple he had not long finished, as dear little Bella bustled about hospitably, making tea and putting some of her cakes on a plate for us.

"They're marvellous, John," I said, as I examined one superb example of his work; "how do you make them?"

"Och, it's no' verra hard. I take the horn of a ram, cut it and heat it and shape it by hand, then polish it. Then I take a piece of hazelwood, one that is good and straight – no bends, you understand, and sand it and then fit it to the horn, then varnish it, and there you have it." John was a humble man.

I examined with admiration the crook he showed me. At the bend of the handle he had carved a small thistle into the sheep's horn.

"And you don't think all that is hard?"

"No, not really, not if ye're careful, you understand."

I thought of the hours of work that had gone into that crook… the patient heating and shaping, bending and carving, the search for just the right length of perfect hazelwood.

"I think you are something of a genius, John. I could never do anything like that in a hundred years – make that two hundred."

"Would you like me to make you one?" asked John.

His words took me completely by surprise. "John, I'd dearly love one, but…"

John broke in quickly. "There'd be no charge. It would be a gift."

"Oh – it's not the thought of the money! I'll happily pay for one. It's your time – all that work!"

"I'll make you one," said John, "and it's a gift. I'll shorten the length, for you're not likely to be wanting it for the sheep. It'll be a fine walker for walking in heather."

A couple of weeks later Janet and I were at Dunbeath and on the way home decided to drop in to see John and Bella.

Bella met us at the door. "Come in, come in," she greeted us cheerily; you'll find John in the lounge room. I'll put on the kettle."

When we walked in to the lounge room, John was waiting for us. "Ah, Lachlan and Janet - how pleasant it is to see you! I was hoping you'd call soon. I have something for you. Sit you doon and I'll fetch it."

As we waited I whispered to Janet, "John must have finished the walker already!"

Soon John was back, holding the walker. "What do you think of it Lachlan?" he asked as he handed it to me.

I held it lovingly, taking in the finely crafted ram's horn handle with its carved thistle; the carefully selected hazelwood shaft. I ran my hand down its length, noting the finish, sanded to perfection and stained. I could hardly believe that John had done all that work to give to me. It crossed my mind that the old shepherd had possibly spent even more time on it than usual.

"John," I said, it's lovely beyond words, and I'll treasure it always. Thank you from the bottom of my heart."

"Ah, thank you, Lachlan, for those kindly words," said the old man; "but that's not the end o' it!"

I stared at him, nonplussed. "I beg your pardon?"

John chuckled as he walked to the corner of the room where he picked up another, identical walker.

"It seemed unfair, not to make one for you too, Janet," he said, offering it to her; "this is for you."

Chapter 9

Parish Visiting

One day we decided to drive again up to John o' Groats, for there is a lot to see around the area there. Just out of Wick there is a turn-off that one should take to the right, which I missed, and we ended up in the pretty village of Castletown before we realised our mistake. No worries – At Castletown one simply turns right and heads east along the top lip of Scotland.

On the way is a turn-off to Dunnet Head, the REAL most northerly point of the British mainland; not John o' Groats as many believe. John o' Groats has the honour, and as there is nothing much at all at Dunnet Head, apart from a lighthouse, it doesn't really matter.

It was a chilly, grey day, so the picnic lunch we brought with us was eaten in the car.

Chilly grey day or no, it is so lovely around John o' Groats, lonely and beautiful in its own way. I took a picture of a gull sitting on a light post on the tiny harbour, watching an Orkney ferry heading for Gills Bay, down past the misty and uninhabited island of Stroma.

On the way back, we passed through the small and pretty village of Keiss, dominated by its ancient castle which, like Dunbeath's, is occupied as a home.

I set about the task of visiting as many as I could in the time left to us in Scotland. I have always seen visiting folk in their own homes as an integral part of the calling of a minister. It is in their homes that a minister gets to know his people; their hopes and fears and worries. He shares those with them as well as their joys and triumphs and so can rejoice with them in the glad days.

Being out and about a lot was a lovely way to watch the advancing spring. As the month drew on, there were signs of spring everywhere. The countryside was greening noticeably. Outside the manse, dozens of ravens were building their nests in trees already sprouting. The burns bubbled merrily on their way to the sea as the snows melted. Gorse tinged the hills with pretty yellow, while many a road and lane was lined with golden daffodils. Shy primroses, hiding among the banks and braes, sprinkled the sweet earth with tiny petals of delicate white.

Not long now, I thought, before all the trees would be clothed in all their summer finery.

The older part of Dunbeath village is quaint, and delightfully so, and half the houses are classified by the Heritage Council.

I had been enjoying my work, finding my way around its few streets and meeting the parishioners who live there. Everyone quite literally knows everyone else.

Others live on crofts and farms; some of them very large and beautiful. Everywhere I went, small cottage or large house, the welcome was the same: warm as the cheery fires that glowed in many a hearth, and almost invariably the teapot was produced. The folk were hospitable indeed.

At one home I visited, the husband greeted me cheerfully and then added, "I cannae find the wife at the moment. She's probably in the sitootery."

Sitootery? I have learned many Scottish words over the years but that was a new one.

We went out to the back of the house where a greenhouse had been converted to a very comfortable sort of a sunroom. Inside I could see a lady reading.

"Ah – there she is!" exclaimed my genial host – "in the sitootery."

After we had chatted for a while I had to ask: "Would you mind telling me the meaning of 'sitootery'?"

They both laughed. "In Australia," my host explained, "you would probably call it a "SIT OUTERY." In other words, a place to sit outside, out of the weather and enjoy the sun!"

All was revealed, and I added that delightful new word to my vocabulary!

We were charmed by the numbers of pretty little villages and hamlets that lie within the bounds of the parish. Some were hidden away and possibly rarely seen by tourists.

We also enjoyed having folk call in on us. We certainly had room to entertain in that elegant and spacious manse.

On our walks around the village Janet and I often detected the unmistakable aroma of peat fires, which we came to recognise in the North Isles of Shetland.

One day I took Janet with me, visiting to the north of our village, around another tiny village called Ulbster, which is part of the parish, but as always one should never travel without a camera. As in Shetland, there are views around every corner.

The sun shone all day and the wind stayed away, and although the temperature stuck stubbornly to a maximum of about ten degrees, it was a great day to be "oot and aboot."

We were getting acclimatised and found ourselves thinking of it as quite a warm day.

Quite by accident, with no idea it was there, we discovered small but lovely loch, called Loch Watenan, which is a wildlife habitat.

Just nearby but right on the cliff-face there are the whalegoe steps, of which George had told me that day in hospital. The steps – 365 of them – disappear down the side of a great cliff, to a sort of make-shift harbour below. On the outer side of the steps there is a sheer drop down a rock face, so sticking closely to the steps is wise.

As we stood at the top, a bearded man stepped out of one of the stone houses nearby and bade us good day. He was a very pleasant man, only too eager, as we have often found, to tell us something of the local history. He explained that he was one who cared for the steps and was full of information. The steps were built, he told us, in 1793 for a cost of £8/-/-.

"The men were kind," he added. "Half way up there is a stone, placed there for the womenfolk, and about waist-high, where the women could rest their loads!"

I had a bit of a surprise when we came home. Some time previously we had applied for a bus pass each. Janet's had come quite quickly, but mine had not.

A letter arrived in the post that told me why. It read: "Thank you for your application for the above scheme. Unfortunately, we are unable to issue you with a card for the following reason: The date of birth indicates that the applicant is too young to be eligible for the scheme." I was gratified in a way to learn I was too young, but puzzled at the same time, for Janet had received her pass without question, and she is younger than I, by about four years. She decided to ring to try to solve the mystery.

I could see her on the phone as she told the woman the problem. Then she waited while the information was retrieved. Then I noted she was giggling, which puzzled me even more.

When she hung up she was laughing. "You are an idiot, Lachlan Ness! The woman told me that the applicant was far too young to apply for such a card because, according to the information supplied, Lachlan Ness is only three months old!"

I stared at her, dumbfounded and completely mystified.

"Don't you see? When you wrote your details on the form we sent off, you put the year of your birth as this year - 2009!"

I shook my head, bemused. Surely that error alone should qualify me for a card!!!

I filled in another form that very day – but had Janet check the details.

On 21 March I recorded in my diary: Today is officially the first day of spring in Britain.

The following day was "Mothering Sunday" or Mothers' Day which in Australia is the first Sunday in May.

Tomorrow, the fourth Sunday of Lent, would indeed be Mothering Sunday.

Chapter 10

Add-on John again

While leaving the manse one morning, I saw Keith, the policeman who lived opposite. He stopped with a hand on his gate and called me over. "Lach, have you heard the latest about Add-on John?"

I hadn't.

"You're not likely to – well, not for a wee while anyway, until things settle down. Addon often stays in Lybster in his small flat as you know, but he also owns the house beside it, which is rented by a fellow who works out on the oil rigs – what they call around here as working offshore. He couldn't understand the big electricity bills he was getting, so the other day he decided to have the wiring checked out – and wasn't he in for a surprise! It seems that Addon had his electricity connected to the tenant's house, so the oil rig man was paying, not only for his own power usage, but Addon's as well! He was not pleased. He's big, and has a short fuse. He wants to sort out Addon, who decided a brief holiday was in order, so left town. He's had to do that once or twice before, as did his father before him. Unfortunately it won't be for long, because the oil rig man is moving down south to one of the rigs off Aberdeen."

"Has Addon a longish history in the district?" I asked.

"Aye – that he has, and his father before him, as I said. Someone once told me that back in the days when there was a milkman to deliver milk around the village, Addon's father was the local milkman. People used to complain about the thinness of the milk and there was a rumour that Addon's dad, known around the toon as 'Tightwad Tony' used to water it down. The rumour blossomed into fact when one day a lady poured her milk into a jug after having it delivered by auld Tightwad and saw something unusual floating in it. When she pulled the object out, she found a dead tadpole! Well, the game was up, y'ken, and the old man disappeared for a while. There was a pond at the bottom of his farm and later it was learned that he used to scoop out a bucket or two each day to mix with the milk, to help stretch it a bit further – and his purse too, of course!"

"It seems," I said, "that his son, young John, was a good apprentice in roguery."

Thursday was World Day of Prayer, held in our Lybster Church in the afternoon.

As we all gathered, I thought of Christians all over the world, in many time zones, who would be gathering for this act of global worship, Christian unity and fellowship. I particularly thought of the folk in our Church back in Australia.

Janet had the job of preaching. The text chosen by the international committee was from the Book of Acts chapter 4, verse 32: "They were one in heart and spirit."

I'd helped her prepare her sermon but she was very nervous. She shouldn't have been, for she preached very well. It was a very encouraging service; a true reminder that we are all one in Christ.

"How did it sound – the sermon?" Janet asked me nervously as we gathered for afternoon tea.

"You were marvellous!" I told her; "God was with you, all the way – and so were we all!"

It had been a bitterly cold day and I was not looking forward to going to the Worship Group meeting at Andrew's and Jean's that evening.

When I went out to get in the car, shivering, despite plenty of warm clothing, I discovered that the windscreen had completely iced over, so spent five minutes blowing hot air from the heater onto the car's windscreen before I could drive off.

The meeting itself was productive, for the Worship Group was to conduct the service on "Mothering Sunday" – what is known in Australia and the USA as "Mothers' Day."

In Britain it's held on the third Sunday in March. It was decided that Lorraine should preach.

After the meeting, when we went out to our cars, all our windscreens were frozen solid. Back at Lybster I noted that the Volkswagen appeared to have an unusual sheen on its paintwork. Curiously I inspected it, to discover that I'd been driving an iceblock.

The car was covered in solid ice. It was quite an experience for one coming from a district where even a frost is quite unusual

Chapter 11

Sadness and gladness

I was busily going over my sermon late one Saturday afternoon in March, when I was called to the phone. It was John, the deacon.

"Lachlan – I'm sorry to have to tell you, but there's been a sudden death in the village! I'm down in Edinburgh at present and can't get back, but I've known the man for quite a long time... Nice fellow. He was found dead in a building he's been renovating. Don't know the details yet. Anyway, he's dead. Would you go to see the widow?" He gave me the name and address.

I left at once, in driving rain and a wild gale, to the new widow's house. She was convulsed with grief. I learned that she and her husband had not been here long and she herself spoke English as a second language, although her husband was Scottish.

I was there for about an hour until friends began to arrive. I knew there would have to be a post mortem and that would delay any funeral service.

When I left the house, out of the darkness of grief, into the gale-lashed blackness with the rain tearing at me, the sense of tragedy lay even more heavily upon my spirit; as if the night itself were tearing its hair in sympathy.

I was back at the house of sorrow the following afternoon. Fortunately the widow, who was very devout, had good friends to support her through that terrible emotional storm. She told me she planned to have the funeral in Inverness, with John officiating.

Friday was Janet's birthday, and was filled with much happiness as she inspected the cards and received numerous phone calls and messages. I gave her a card and a nice McGowans "Highland Toffee," which proved to be a bit sweet for her, so I was forced to eat it myself. I could not bear the thought of wasting the 10p.

In the evening, I took the birthday girl to "The Portland Arms" hotel for dinner, a three minute walk from the manse and a really great place to dine. I had been fascinated to learn that it had been a staging place where the coaches arrived to change horses on their journey south or north. In my mind I could imagine the coach and four thundering into the village, top-hatted driver at the reins, huddled into his greatcoat, hat pulled low, as the assistant gives a warning blast on the horn. The coach pulls up outside the inn. See the horses, steam from their hot flanks and nostrils rising in the cold air, being unharnessed as fresh horses wait, while the merry passengers, glad to be there, stamp their feet on the frosty ground and move in to the inn for a meal and an ale before resuming their journey.

The interior of the Portland Arms these days is still old-fashioned and lovely, with lots of warm wood panels. There is an open fire and a huge AGA stove, in which some of the meals are cooked.

After a tasty meal, we moved down to the lounge area; so very old-world and beautifully furnished in traditional style, where we had coffee ("We don't do cappuccinos – only proper coffee" we were told), which arrived on a tray in a silver coffee pot. We sat there and drank the coffee and as well drank in the superb atmosphere… no pokies, no crowds, no garish music… two or three dining couples, quietness and peace, and all for a total of £24.00.

Back at the manse, I received an email letter from our friend Lis in the North Isles of Shetland, where I'd been a locum minister the previous year.

Lis knows more about the English language and its origins than anyone else I know. I must have mentioned Spittal in a recent letter to her, which is the name of a little Caithness village we had passed through one day. In her reply Lis wrote:

"Spittal is short for HOSPITAL, usually ancient monastic establishments long ago for the lodging and care of travellers. 'Hostel' and 'Hotel' come from the same root… they are often in out-of-the-way places, and often with no obvious buildings for the eye of the stranger to notice today. The Spittal of Glenshee is high up in the mountains on the A93, where they ski today. There is a Spittal on the opposite side (south side) of the river Tweed from Berwick-on-Tweed. Now you have found another one!"

I had mentioned to Lis that Janet and I had gone to a bulb show in Wick, where cakes were also judged, and I was intrigued by several cakes being judged called simnel cakes. It seems there is a fascinating story behind the simnel cake too.

Let me quote Lis again:

"Simnel cake is traditional on Mothering Sunday, the mid-Sunday of Lent. On this day, servants were traditionally allowed home to their parents and to their Mother-Church, where they had been baptised. Their employers gave them the wherewithal to bake this cake to take home. The marzipan top has ELEVEN marzipan balls, one for each of the disciples, minus one for Judas Iscariot. The OED says that the derivation is SIMILA (Latin) – the finest flour! There is a layer of marzipan cooked in the middle of the cake, too. The spices reflect the spices used to embalm the body…"

Hiding behind our Christian faith are so many remarkable stories, and I thank Lis for making those two known to me, which I happily pass on to you, and I am sure you also will be fascinated.

Chapter 12

The Kisting

The death of John Mac, one of the elders of the parish, did not come as a complete surprise, but when it did, it brought a great deal of sorrow, for he was loved by his family and widely respected and admired in the community.

Janet and I had been to visit John and his charming wife Margaret, where we enjoyed their warm hospitality, and were just getting to know them well.

John was from the island of Lewis, in the Hebrides, and in many ways his heart was still there. He spoke Gaelic perfectly and also taught it. When he first came to the mainland, he said, he knew no English; only Gaelic. He was gifted with a naturally warm and engaging personality that drew people to him, and as we discovered, also had a marvellous sense of humour. He also possessed a very strong faith that served him well.

Both he and Margaret were devout Christians and members of the Lybster congregation.

At first, John's admission to the Wick hospital did not seem to be too much of a concern, although he had a terribly rattly chest, accompanied by a severe cough. I went in to see him and always left smiling, for he could see the funny side of just about any situation, but he always liked to finish my visits with a prayer.

Suddenly, John was transferred to the big hospital in Inverness as his condition deteriorated. I was thankful that John the deacon could visit him there. John Mac himself may have had an inkling that the end was approaching, for one day three elders arrived at the hospital from Lewis, who could pray with him in the Gaelic.

Not long after, John the deacon dropped in to tell me that John's life support had been switched off, and later that evening, Pauline the session clerk rang to tell me that he had died.

Next morning, I drove out to see Margaret, who was deep in grief. Two of her daughters had arrived to be with their mother, and the rest of the family were due.

"Och well," commented Margaret through her tears, "The good news is that he knew who he was and Whose he was, and there's no greater comfort than that."

We discussed the service around the table. "Margaret, I said, "I think it's only fitting that John the deacon should conduct the service. After all, he's known you, John and your family for years and as well, he's an old friend."

When I left, we had most of the service sorted out.

That afternoon, John the deacon dropped by for tea and a chat.

"Lachlan," John said, reaching for a biscuit, "have you ever heard of a Kisting?"

I had not.

"A Kisting is a traditional service," he explained, "originally from the Western Isles but certainly not unknown here. It goes like this: A day or two before the funeral service, the deceased is brought in the coffin to the house of the bereaved. A service is held there around his remains, and that's what a Kisting is. A kist is a Gaelic word and it originally meant a 'chest' of the sort that men would carry on their shoulders, such as a sea-kist. In time, the word came to be identified as a coffin. Sometimes the funeral is held in the house, and the coffin (or kist) leaves from there for the graveyard, while on other occasions the coffin is taken from the house to the church for the service. Anyway, John's family wants a Kisting, but requests the main service to be held in the church, which is good news. There will be a lot of people who'll want to pay their respects."

"I hope that you'll conduct this Kisting, John. I've never heard of the word, let alone know what sort of a service it is!"

The deacon smiled and looked at my face. "No need to be alarmed, Lachlan - of course I'll conduct the service – I've done so several times before. By the way, I've asked Jim Morrison, the Free Church of Scotland man to be there too. He's known the family for years. The three of us can take part in the service."

The following evening we gathered at the family home. All the family had arrived, including family members from Lewis and Harris in the Hebrides.

Shortly after our arrival the funeral directors arrived with John's kist, placed it reverently on its stand in a spare room and removed the lid. John looked very much at peace.

We were all very subdued. John the deacon commenced the Service which included a brief sermon, followed by Jim the Free Church man who offered a prayer and a reading, while I finished with a prayer and the Benediction. It was a very comforting, simple service.

Later, as we joined the family over supper, John the deacon told me that the kist would remain there, open, and members of the family would be free to visit the room to recall the past and offer a prayer of thanksgiving for John's life.

John and Margaret had been blessed with three marvellous daughters who had arrived with husbands and children to take over from their mother.

I was pleased to have Jim the Free Church man there as well, for he was a tower of strength. He and his wife Cathy, Janet and I had become good friends.

On Saturday morning, after the funeral Service in the Lybster Church, John was laid to rest at Mid-Clyth, a walled cemetery overlooking the sea.

There were so many cars that a policeman had to be put on point duty at the cemetery turn-off.

The weather reflected the mood of many: a haar (fog) had descended, and when it lifted, it was replaced by drizzle. Fortunately Margaret was surrounded by the love of her daughters, their families and children, as well as many other family members and friends in the Church and community.

Afterwards, Janet and I joined the mourners at the "Portland Arms" for hot tomato soup and sandwiches.

It was pleasing to see how she was surrounded by that loving family, but soon a few of those who had come from so far away, had to leave.

The writer of Ecclesiastes said, "There is a time to be born and a time to die. A time to weep and a time to laugh" (3:2,4. NIV) and after John's sad death, followed by the Kisting and funeral, and affected a little as I was by the grief of the family, it occurred to me that "a time to laugh" would be beneficial.

It came in the form of something Lorraine, one of the elders wrote, to be included in the following Sunday's Order of Service.

It read: The Sunday School and Youth Groups are in need of more people on the rota for Sunday mornings at Lybster Church. If you need a good excuse to miss a few sermons, please contact... (rota = roster in Australia).

I loved her sense of humour, and the easy sense of humour of so many of the folk there. I couldn't help thinking that the notice would certainly rattle the confidence of a few of the more humourless ministers I've met over the years, some of whom would be outraged and deeply offended, but as the writer of the Book of Proverbs put it, "A cheerful heart is good medicine . . ." (17:22a. NIV).

Chapter 13

Easter, jelly beans and egg rolling

In Australia, Easter arrives during autumn, when the days are cooling after a long, hot summer. It's the loveliest season of the year, looked forward to by most as a relief from summer's heat. As the season deepens, there is little wind, the days are mild and the sun shines.

Up in the far north of Scotland, it's different. Easter arrives in spring, when the weather is unstable and never hot.

It certainly was not hot during the Easter of 2009, in the parish of Latheron. Good Friday was decidedly the opposite, and I was grateful I didn't have an early morning service; in fact the only service I had to prepare for was an evening Service.

During the afternoon Eileen from the shop, wonderful person that she was, arrived at the manse with two very large containers of soup – enough to last a day or three. A marvellous cook, she was forever baking and cooking, usually for others, many of them the less fortunate in the community.

In the evening, Lybster church was half-full of Good Friday worshippers, and as usual Pat the organist and the Jabos singers led our hymns, and sang a moving anthem, all of which helped make it a memorable service.

Over the preceding days I had been looking about for a suitable Easter Day story for the children and one day I found it. It was a little verse called The Jelly Bean Poem. In the poem, a jelly bean of each colour is held up to represent a part of the Easter story. It was a delightful little poem so I decided to use it, but rather than use someone else's work, sat down to write my own (which I hereby make freely available to anyone who may be reading this book and would like to use my version of the jelly bean poem).

The discovery of the jelly bean poem also presented me with an ideal opportunity to indulge my craving. I decided to make certain that the quantity purchased would be more than the quantity to be consumed, and I had plans for the left-overs…

The reason for the odd decision is sad to relate. I had become irretrievably addicted to the giant jelly beans sold in the shop by Eileen's husband Eric.

The shopkeeper became used to seeing me slink furtively and hurriedly into the shop with an order: "Quick, Eric – a quarter pound of the usual. Janet is over at the newsagency, picking up the John O' Groat Journal – and, um, there's no need to mention this little transaction to her. What the eye doesn't see, and all that…"

Each of those visits produced a reaction in Eric. Invariably he rolled his eyes to heaven before reaching up behind the counter to fetch down the large bottle crammed with jelly beans.

Janet knew of the addiction and was concerned for my health, even after I had explained to her, patiently and many times, that jelly beans have lots of sugar, thus providing me with the energy I required for my duties. They also have preservatives, thereby helping me to keep my boyish looks (even I blushed at that outrageous porkie) and the bright colours are great for warding off depression. Janet was not convinced. Each time, Eric's head shook reprovingly as he carefully weighed the beans on an old-fashioned set of scales before pouring them into a paper bag: "Och, you're drawing me intae a conspiracy Lachlan. One day we're going tae get caught. Dinnae say I have nae warned you…"

On Easter morning we were at Dunbeath for the 10.00am service. Because Dunbeath is much smaller than Lybster, the attendances were also smaller, but we had become very close to that warm and friendly Dunbeath congregation.

At 11.30 I was in the pulpit of the Lybster Church, which was packed and included visitors from various places.

There were quite a few children in attendance. I had numerous small bags of jelly beans with me, and each bag had the various coloured jelly beans I needed for the children's story.

When it came time for the children's story I recited my poem as I held up each coloured bean:

Blood - red stands for the life He gave;
While green tells us of the empty grave.
Orange is for a new day dawning;
Yellow, the sun on Easter morning.
A black bean stands for the wrong we've done;
And white for forgiveness, through God's Son.
Purple tells of His grief and pain;
While blue tells us that He rose again.
A jelly bean is a tasty sweet;
Pretty to look at, delicious to eat.
We can use our colourful jelly beans
To tell us truly what Easter means.

At the end of the talk I had three of the children, Steven, Chloe and Rachel hand a bag of beans containing the relevant coloured beans, and a copy of the poem, to each of the other children, Pat the organist and the Jabos singers led us in the music and congregational singing, and we were treated to a glorious and triumphant anthem by the Jabos singers.

All of us felt uplifted at the end of the service, and I looked forward eagerly to a surreptitious treat of left-over jelly beans...

Earlier in the week I'd mentioned to Janet that during the Easter Day afternoon I thought it appropriate that we visit John Mac's widow, Margaret. John had died not long before Easter and his funeral had included the Kisting. Margaret, her daughters and families, were all at the Easter service, so I knew she would be at home. Margaret was always in church, but her family lived further south, either in Scotland or in England, but were up to spend more time with their mother who was still in mourning.

We arrived in mid-afternoon and Margaret met us at the door.

"Most of the family are up the hill, egg-rolling," she told us; "In fact they're waiting for you."

A few days earlier someone I'd been visiting asked me if I'd be doing any egg-rolling over Easter. I was just about to ask what it was, when the phone rang, and my host had to go, and I left. Now I was about to find out.

Margaret's property was an acreage, and when we looked up the hill we could see figures, and they were waving to us.

We were puffing when finally we made it, and there was dark-eyed Barbara, her husband and the children behind her, coming to greet us, all holding brightly painted hard-boiled eggs.

Up there on the hill, the wind was chilly but exhilarating. It was a glorious day. The sun shone from a cloudless sky, and we had a superb view over the North Sea, all sparkling and blue.

"Welcome! So glad you could make it! called Barbara; "Have you been egg-rolling before?"

We shook our heads. "What is it?" Janet asked.

Barbara smiled. "Watch us!"

The family stood in a row on the top of the hill and as we watched, rolled their eggs down the slope. We watched them as they bounced and wobbled their way over tufts of grass and peat. Little Isla jumped up and down excitedly as the eggs rolled to a stop.

"I won! I won!" she yelled.

The family went down to collect the eggs. Zoe, the older daughter, handed us each a painted egg. "The trick," she explained, "is to see who can roll their egg the farthest, without breaking it."

We had a practice go. Janet showed some promise as an egg roller, but my efforts were not good.

We spent the rest of the afternoon, rolling our eggs, and the excitement generated rivalled that of the Melbourne Cup.

Finally, we all came down to the house for a welcome tea, coffee and some of Margaret's cakes.

"There's plenty more, so eat up," Margaret told us. "The folk have been marvellous, since John died. We've been given so much food. I won't have to cook for ages."

"What is the origin of the egg rolling tradition, Margaret?" I asked.

"It goes back a long way, Lachlan, and symbolises the rolling away of the stone from the door of the tomb on Easter morning."

We were quite tired as we drove home after a most exhilarating and exciting afternoon with that wonderful family.

"It never ceases to amaze me," I remarked as we drove, "how many of those old traditions, such as egg rolling, have their roots in the Christian faith."

Janet nodded. "It's true. Who knows – one day the jelly bean poem may become a tradition."

A sudden thought struck me. "Speaking of jelly beans; did you happen to find some that were left over? They were in a large bag, in the study. I looked for them before we left."

"Find some that were left over? You must be kidding!" There was an exasperated edge to Janet's voice: "I found enough jelly beans to fill a shopping trolley! You really miscalculated the number of children you expected at that service today, Lachlan!"

"And the jelly beans... Are they still in the study?"

"What? Of course not! While you were out on one of your visiting afternoons, I bought many more bags, filled them all with jelly beans, and today I handed them out, together with copies of the poem, to the congregations at the door of each church! Surely you saw me?"

I hadn't. I drove home in glum silence. Janet thought I was tired.

"We've had a long day," she said.

Chapter 14

A bit of this and a bit of that

As we greeted the folk coming out the church after the service one Sunday, one of the ladies sighed and said "Och – the year is running away. In no time at all it will be the tattie holidays."

"What," I asked, "are the tattie holidays?"

"They're the October holidays," she explained. "At one time all the children had to have holidays in October to help gather in the tatties (potato harvest) and the October holidays still go by that name."

Caithness has its own unique dialect although, unlike Shetland, it's not so much spoken these days.

I was always on the on the lookout for new words. One that caught my ear was the word "teuchter" which I heard one day when taking the religious instruction class at Dunbeath school. The children were always interested in Australia and on this occasion, one child asked me where I had grown up.

"In Leeton, in the south-west of New South Wales," I replied. "It's a long way from the city. It's farming country down that way."

"Och, then, you're a teuchter?" ventured Meghan, who often used a lot of unusual words.

I stared at her. "A teuchter? What's a teuchter?"

"It's a . . . I don't know how to say it," Meghan replied, after a couple of starts.

The teacher broke in. "A teuchter is a sort of countryman – a farming type who lives in the country – a bit like a rustic I suppose. I don't know what the Australian term is."

"A bushie," I said. "A bushie is someone who lives in the bush, or was brought up in the bush, which doesn't mean in some garden bush. It means a place well out of any city. Yes, Meghan is right. I'm a teuchter!" The children laughed, and I had to smile. Meghan was a very amusing child with a funny sense of humour.

On another occasion when Meghan was speaking, I had no idea what she was saying. Finally the teacher intervened. "Meghan – speak English!" she told her crossly. Meghan had been speaking in the Caithness dialect.

In the Dunbeath school staff room at morning tea one day I told the staff of a Scottish teacher I had as a boy in Australia. His standard response to some wildly improbable answer to a question he posed was a theatrical groan followed by "Ness, yer brains are in yer boots and yer boots are left at hame!" The Dunbeath staff were amused, but no one appeared prepared to adopt the saying.

The Latheron Show

The following day we went off to the Latheron Show, which was held in a field not far from Lybster. It was a tiny country show, similar to the ones in Australia, and was marvellous. We wandered about the grounds, admiring pens of exotic-looking chooks (Australian and New Zealand word for fowls, hens or chickens), sheep, goats, cattle. All had been judged and the winners had their ribbons tied to their pens - all except the goats, which had a penchant for eating theirs, which were on the ground in front. There were parades of beautiful horses and ponies, from Clydesdales to Shetlands as well as dressage competitions. There were other stalls of course, with fairy floss (what the locals called candy floss), hamburgers and other culinary desirables. Whole tents were filled with the most beautiful craft work, cooking and baking.

Janet bought a bucket of chips, which we ate as we walked about in the chill wind that blew across leaden skies. It was all the fun of the fair but we had to leave, for at 3.00pm we were to be at a wedding down at the little Latheronwheel Harbour.

"O Happy Wedding Day"

The happy couple, Tony and Gay, were members of our congregation: Tony was ex-Royal Navy so wore his uniform jacket with Black Watch kilt and looked very handsome, while Gay looked lovely in her wedding gown.

John the deacon, tall and resplendent in tartan trews, officiated, and did that excellently.

A couple of youngsters piped and many men were kilted.

It was freezing down at Latheronwheel harbour, with an icy wind blowing straight in off the North Sea.

Gay and her bridesmaids shivered. Janet very sensibly wore the overcoat that Jean from St John's Waratah-Mayfield had loaned her before we left. Some of the others, in frilly summer outfits, froze. "It's lovely, cuddling you, Janet!" one of the more scantily dressed ladies exclaimed, laughing, as she hugged her; "You're the only lady with a warm coat!"

We went along to the magnificent wedding reception at the "Portland Arms." It was quite a memorable evening.

Chapter 15

The flight of the bumbling Lachlan, with bee

The whole parish had been looking forward to the Confirmation Service. It was to be a very special one indeed. The usual practice was to combine the Dunbeath & Lybster congregations on the first Sunday of the month, but this one was to be memorable, for it was the first time in years when there would be confirmations.

As I stood in the pulpit at the commencement of the service I looked out upon a sea of shining faces, which included visitors from England and New Zealand.

I announced the first hymn and the congregation rose as one to sing the triumphal Psalm 24, verses 7 to 10, to the lovely tune St George's Edinburgh. The singing was led by Pat at the organ and our little Jabos choir.

The confirmations were very moving for those participating, and there were tears, hugs and kisses among the newly confirmed and their families, as well as some of the congregation.

The confirmation service was followed by Communion, and afterwards, we all adjourned to the church hall for tea and sticky buns, so it was something of a gala day.

A week after the Latheron Agricultural Show was held, it was the turn of the Annual Wick Agricultural Show, so Janet and I went.

I was interested to see a display of vintage tractors, and the most popular among them was the famous old Ferguson. The owners had brought them in for the general public to admire, and I was among the admirers. They looked as good if not better than they did when new, back in the 1950's.

The original Ferguson tractor was grey, but later ones were red. My father had a grey one, powered by kerosene which in those days was cheaper than petrol, and my brother Bill could drive it like a veteran when he was seven years old. To reach the clutch, he had to jump off the seat to push it down with his foot, for he was only wee, then shove the gearstick into the next gear, then leap back on the seat again.

Nowadays we know it was highly dangerous, but back then life was much more casual. One slip and he would have been under those big back wheels. Little Bill however was both practical and intelligent and would have made a great farmer, had the land been for him.

My father tried his hardest to teach my mother to drive the Fergy, usually with disastrous but occasionally hilarious results.

My poor mother - she hated anything mechanical and to the day she died would not use even a potato peeler, but always used a knife, and not being particularly dextrous, took several centimetres of potato as she peeled. Well-covered, fat potatoes were reduced to weedy thin naked ones by the time my mother had them ready for the pot.

As our children grew, my mother occasionally knitted them sweaters, but could never get the head-holes right. She made them so tiny that our cat would have had trouble getting his head through, and on the odd occasion when we forced the head of one of our children into the tiny opening, getting the sweater off again was to risk having an earless child.

Janet quietly gave the sweaters to her mother, an excellent knitter, and she made them wearable.

To his dying day my father could never really accept the fact that he had an impractical wife and eldest son.

I was very glad my father was not there to witness an incident that occurred a couple of days after the Annual Wick show. I was in my study, going over the next Sunday's Order of Service when Janet walked in. "Lachlan, a bee is in the lounge room. Would you please remove it?" Killing insects or spiders that wander into our house is not an option for me. I always remove them and release them.

I have perfected a means of rescue and release of small flying visitors that manage to get into the house and then want to get out, but find it impossible. They can't understand clear glass and why they can't get forward motion.

I brought in my usual tools of trade: a clear plastic container and a sheet of paper. The first part went well enough. I placed the plastic cup over the bee, which was buzzing futilely against the window, slid the sheet of paper underneath, then turned the cup upside down, bee inside, with the paper acting as a lid to contain it. The next part of the operation was to take the bee outside and release it.

As I turned to leave, the usual Ness clumsiness asserted itself. One shoe caught in a coffee table behind me, which unbalanced me. I flew like an out of control Dumbo the flying elephant across the room, crashed into a second coffee table and would have hit my head on a wooden inset of the armchair upon which Janet was seated, had she not deftly put her hand there, thus cushioning my head with her hand.

I lay on the floor groaning and bleeding as Janet, the former nursing sister Ness, tended my wounds. (She gets quite a bit of practice). I could feel warm blood running down my temple and see some more good A Negative seeping through my trouser leg at the knee.

"A miracle!" I croaked suddenly.

"A miracle you didn't brain yourself!" was Janet's terse response as she applied a bandage.

"No!" I insisted – a real miracle! Look!" She looked.

In all that chaos of plunging body and crashing coffee tables, with contents flying everywhere, I'd held the bee in the cup, the sheet of paper still over the mouth of it, all the way to the floor! The container was split, but it held together enough for Janet to release the bee into the garden, which I implored her to do before returning to tend my injuries. Bees deprived of nectar don't live long.

The next day there was to be a service at the Lybster school, involving Jim the Free Church man, John the deacon and myself.

"I don't know if I can make it," I said to Janet as I got ready to go. "I can hardly walk this morning. That leg won't take the weight."

"Why not take the walker stick that John the shepherd made you?" she suggested. It was a good idea.

As I was about to leave, the walker at my side, I turned to Janet. "How do I look?" I asked.

She examined me briefly and replied. "Crumpled," then added kindly, "but that's the way you are."

I didn't like to ask if she was referring to my clothes or my face.

With the walker taking most of the weight, I limped the short distance from the manse to the school, very much aware of the stiff and swollen knee.

I arrived at the same time as John the deacon.

The deacon stared at the apparition limping painfully towards him.

His gaze went from the walker to my bandaged head. "Hullo – what happened to you, Lachlan – were you run over by a bus?"

"A bee did it," I told him.

John gave me a look. It was the look I'd seen from time to time on the face of my father...

Chapter 16

Down the Strath and up the Glen

With the advancing spring making outdoors work a lot more pleasant, visiting my parishioners became quite a pleasant exercise.

During one week my visiting took me from down near Berriedale in the south, up to Bruan in the north, which were more or less the polar boundaries of the parish.

It was exhilarating, being out and about, travelling the winding roads in that diesel-sipping VW Golf, seeing all manner of folk, and invariably being made welcome.

Everywhere beautiful little lambs were starting to skip about in fields where daisies grow. It was charming to see them, so full of life and fun, gambolling, or trotting contentedly beside their mothers. There were many twins among them. As well as the sheep, there were many new foals and calves. Occasionally, on the wooded hills, there were shy deer with their fawns.

It was near lunch time one day when I was arrived at a lonely crofter's house. My knock on the door was met by the crofter's wife, accompanied by a gracious invitation to enter. As we sat and chatted over a cup of tea I could see lunch bubbling away in a pot on the stove. Occasionally the lady got up to stir it. Finally, looking out through the window she commented, "Here comes Bob noo – coming in fae his porridge. There's plenty, so you are welcome to stay."

Porridge is my staple breakfast food, and I love it, but I politely declined, for I had more visits to make before dusk.

As I drove away I recalled being told that the old herring fishermen had a diet of porridge, for it sticks to the ribs, warms the cockles of the heart, builds bonnie bouncing babies and is probably responsible for many other metaphors, mixed and otherwise.

The old ways are the best ways for these folk. A year or so ago, one of the multi-national fast-food chains opened in Wick. It lasted about three months or so and then left, never to be seen again. The nearest of those types of fast food places is 'way doon in Inverness', but here at the little cafe and takeaway in Lybster's main street, one can enjoy, among other things, (including the finest local salmon and chips), haggis and chips.

One evening I gave a talk on police chaplaincy in Australia to the Wick Rotary Club. John the deacon had been interested to hear that back in Australia, I am still a parttime police chaplain. After retirement, I didn't give it up.

It was John, who belonged to Wick Rotary Club, who had invited me to be guest speaker, and for Janet and me to accompany him and Pauline as their guests.

The venue was McKay's hotel in Wick, known far and wide for its superb food and service.

After a warm welcome by our genial Rotary hosts, followed by a fine meal, I stood to speak. Drawing on experiences as a police chaplain in both Queensland and New South Wales, I concentrated on some of the more humorous stories. I'd been nervous about giving the talk. The Australian brand of humour is not always understood in other places around the globe, but the Wick Rotarians seemed to be switched on to it. I was rewarded with many a hearty guffaw, and as we drove home, Janet, John and Pauline said it went over well.

Andrew and Jean, members of the Lybster congregation, lived in a lovely old home with their dog Watson, a whippet. The expression "as thin as a whippet" applied aptly to Watson, but he was well-fed, well-loved and exactly as whippets are meant to be, with a friendly disposition.

The views from the house were spectacular, across rolling fields of deepest green, to where green meets blue, or sometimes grey or sometimes almost black – whatever happened to be the mood of the North Sea at the time.

One day we called in and sat and chatted with them as the late afternoon sun warmed us through the protective glass of their conservatory. Watson's head was on my knee and I was stroking it when Andrew suddenly said, "Would you and Janet like to go on a sight-seeing trip with Jean and me?"

Janet in particular jumped at the idea. She has an insatiable thirst for exploring new areas.

"Whereabouts would you like to take us, Andrew?" I asked.

Andrew smiled and tapped the side of his nose. "Let's see where the car takes us." Andrew, a school teacher, had worked in forestry for years before that, and knew Caithness like the back of his hand. As well, he enjoyed as his recreation finding high mountains and climbing them. We'd been intrigued to learn that in Scotland, mountains are often referred to as "Munros" to distinguish them from hills. Years ago, we were told, a man named Munro had measured every high hill and mountain in Scotland in order to discover which are hills and which are mountains. The name "Munro" is now largely associated with what are real mountains.

The four of us set off one fine morning in our hosts' car, accompanied by Watson. We headed south, where we'd been ourselves, but we were in for a surprise.

Our first stop was at the delightfully pretty village of Berriedale which, like so much of Scotland, is picture- postcard beautiful, and full of history, much of it linked to the Duke of Portland, who owns, we were told, a great deal of property around that area.

From there we travelled on to Helmsdale where we had lunch. Helmsdale, summer or winter, is a beautiful village. It has such a pretty harbour and the village itself is quaint and fascinating, set as it is in the midst of the hills. Andrew drove us down to the harbour, where there were several small boats tied up. I smiled at the name on one bow: Highland Home.

The last time Janet and I had been to Helsmsdale, on our first exploratory trip, it had been quite cold, with snow about, but this time the weather was mild – even warmish for that time of the year at around 8 or 9 degrees. The sun beamed down from a gloriously blue sky, contrasting with the bright yellow gorse on the high hills.

Andrew took the narrow road along the strath of Kildonan with its wooded hills and valleys on one side and the winding Helmsdale river on the other.

"Look!" called Janet, "wild deer!" Andrew slowed the car where two red deer, with mighty antlers, regarded us impassively from the edge of the woods.

Andrew and Jean stopped here and there at places that we had not noticed on our previous trip, or had been too cold to get out of the car.

Up the winding strath we drove, over old stone bridges and around spectacular hills as Andrew pointed out many things, telling us something of the district's past history, until we arrived at a district called Kirkton, where there is nothing but an ancient church with its graveyard, and all about, magnificent, timeless hills.

Further on, we turned off the strath and headed into much remoter country where a signpost pointed to Glen Loth. Janet and I were now in country new to us. It was wild and remote and lovely, with many shades of brown, of peat and sleeping heather and also yellow gorse. It is a vast place, with little evidence of human intrusion.

We stopped at one spot by a burn where Andrew told us an Australian had discovered gold. There had been a brief rush, but no gold of much consequence was found. As usual, the people selling picks, shovels and provisions made the most out of it. To this day, however, people do a bit of panning in the burn and come up with traces of gold. We'd have passed that spot, unaware, had not Andrew and Jean stopped to show us.

We drove up along a very narrow road, one car wide, around great hills and over burns gurgling through the hills, flowing down towards the distant Helmsdale river. The further we travelled, the remoter became the country.

At one spot Andrew stopped the car. "There are deer on that far ridge," he said, pointing.

I could just make out distant blobs that could have been rocks, but the telephoto lens revealed that they were indeed deer. "They're understandably shy," Andrew told us, "for there are men with rifles and 'scopes who want to kill them, and you'll find that venison is readily available in any highland butcher shop."

We'd been travelling in a giant loop. Finally, we came out again on the A9, well south of Helmsdale. As we turned into the A9 Andrew pointed to a sign on the other side of the road. "The sign says that it was about there that the last wolf in Scotland was killed," he told us.

I felt slightly sick at heart at that point.

A short drive to the south was the village of Brora "where," said Andrew, "they make what is arguably the best ice-cream in Scotland. I think we should try some." It was a fitting way to end what had been a remarkable adventure.

As we drove north again, up the A9, we passed the sign near where it's claimed the last wolf in Scotland was killed.

We were all a little tired from our day out, and as we drove in silence I couldn't help thinking of that sign and the loss of a whole species from Scotland. Some may well rejoice, but I felt sorrow. I also reflected sadly, that we Australians have nothing to be proud of, with the extinction of the Tasmanian Tiger and countless other species of flora and fauna on our consciences, and others under threat. The last of anything being killed off, or even being wantonly killed, grieves me.

The human race cold-bloodedly destroys anything that gets in its way. I don't think we were ever meant to be like that. I think God made us to be stewards of the earth, not the destroyers of His creation.

I cheered a little when I remembered that it had been only a day or two before, while visiting a croft, that I'd heard an interesting story. It seems that an eccentric Scottish multi-millionaire is talking about re-introducing wolves into Scotland!

Having seen some of the wild, uninhabited country this side of Scotland, with much more of it over on the western side, I think there is room for them.

Chapter 17

John the Deacon's farewell

A few days later we joined a large crowd of locals in the Lybster village hall for a Ceilidh (Gaelic: a party) which was a concert to thank John the deacon on the eve of his retirement. The gaily decorated hall was packed, and it was a most pleasant evening, of the sort to be found in country areas anywhere – except that this evening was very Scottish, which of course is what could be expected in Highland Scotland.

The evening commenced with a small boy aged nine marching in, playing the bagpipes. He was exceptionally talented. Later he told me he had commenced at the age of six.

That set the tone for the whole evening. Young, kilted lassies danced to the pipes, a local played the accordion, which included a song he'd written in honour of John. The JABOS singers from our Lybster church sang, and a young lassie aged about nine or so recited a poem in the Caithness dialect, about the dreaded midge, which had those who understood Caithness dialect in stitches. There were funny skits and poems, and many words of appreciation spoken regarding John's work in the community and the church.

To add a touch of international flavour, I recited an Australian poem, "A Bush Christening" by Banjo Paterson, but was a little disappointed at its reception. I think I recited it well enough, but the Australian brand of humour isn't really understood by many, I have discovered, and I noted slightly blank looks when I started:

On the outer barcoo, where churches are few...

The barcoo bit and the accent, was a puzzle to them at the very start, but there was a bit of a giggle in other places.

It was a great farewell to John, who intended to keep working, but as a retired deacon.

John and Pauline, Janet and I found ourselves at a table having a bit of time together as our thoughts ranged ahead to the coming days, and the difficulties the parish faced without a called minister.

Pauline sighed. "I feel so worried for the parish, Lachlan," she said. "It's been good, having you and Janet here but there's still no sign of a minister interested in a call to the parish."

I nodded. "It's been very hard, I know, but it would have been a lot worse if it were not for you and John and the Worship committee, two top organists in Pat and Judy, and two very loyal congregations. I think the main thing to remember is not to accept just anyone who shows an interest, but who may be entirely unsuited, for a variety of reasons. Someone like that could destroy this parish."

John's expression was a trifle glum. "I know what you're saying, Lachlan, but it has been hard for us. I suppose we'll just keep going. I feel positive God is working on this too."

"I suppose you've seen it," I said; "someone whom a congregation called out of desperation, who ended up wrecking it. I know I have. It's sad, but it happens."

Janet had been listening in. "Of course, there are times when something so amazing happens, it seems only God could have had a hand in it. Remember the case of Horace Beetson, Lach?"

Pauline looked at each of us in turn. "What happened?"

"Well, it's a bit of a long story I suppose," I said, "but it's a good 'un. I was in the Australian Army at the time, as a chaplain, and posted interstate. We worshipped at the local Presbyterian Church, and its situation was not much different from yours here. It had been vacant for years. I was able to take quite a few services for them of course for I didn't have a parish. One day the session clerk rang me to tell me they'd had an expression of interest from a Rev Horace Beetson, and did I know him?

I knew him well enough, but as I didn't belong to the parish where we worshipped or even that Presbytery, I had no voice. I had little time for Horace, who was a 'wheeler and dealer' as they say. He was known to work the system for all it was worth, was lazy, and something of a glutton – in fact his nickname was "Fang." I had serious reservations about his suitability for that parish, but ethically I could say little. The congregation had to decide. Finally they decided to ask him to preach for a call. The service was at 11.00am, but as he had to leave immediately afterwards, it was arranged to have morning tea beforehand, so that people could meet him, ask him questions and so on.

Horace could really turn on the charm when he wanted to and he impressed everyone. He was seated near me, for we knew each other. Not long before it was time to move into the church for the service, a lady came up to the table and handed me a tin of those English boiled lollies – the ones in the round tins. They're very nice. "Thanks for looking after the dog yesterday for me, Lach," she said; "Betsy (the dog) sends her regards."

Horace's eyes were fixed on the tin. "Would you mind if I have one?" he asked; "My throat is rather dry and I'll be in the pulpit soon."

It was a reasonable request so I handed him the tin - and before my very eyes, he scooped out about ten of them, thanked me and headed for the vestry. It was pure Beetson, that little exchange and I remembered praying, "Lord, this is a marvellous little congregation. Please don't let Horace wreck it."

The service started, and every couple of minutes, I saw Horace surreptitiously stuff one of my lollies into his capacious mouth.

Suddenly, half way through the service, he stopped, and I saw a look of utter horror cross his face. We waited. He seemed to be staring fixedly at the back wall. Suddenly he yelled "Everybody out – out of the church!" We stared at him, speechless. Nobody moved. He yelled again, more urgently "Out! Out!" and pointed to the back door. People started to file out. 'I think he's gone mad!' I heard several people say. It certainly was unlike Horace. Thinking to please or appease, we all filed out and waited. Horace didn't appear. I looked in. He had vanished. All we could do was stare at one another. Someone exclaimed, "His car's just left the car park!" and it had. When we went back in, the only thing we could find unusual was a big pool of water in the toilet which was in a washroom off the vestry.

Well, it seems God had answered my prayer, but not as I thought he would. Horace didn't return any calls. We were all completely mystified. Of course after that, no one wanted a call extended to Horace.

It was Janet who put her finger on the probable reason for Horace's odd behaviour . . ."

Pauline and John stared at each of us. "Well," said John, "Don't keep us in suspense! What was the reason?"

Janet was smiling her mysterious smile.

"That evening," I continued, "as we discussed the strange business at home, Janet said to me, 'I think Horace may have had an accident.'

"An accident?" I asked, rather bewildered, as you can imagine; "What do you mean, an accident? I didn't hear of any accident."

"In his pants." she said. "He couldn't do anything in front of us. He had to get us all out of the church first before he could take himself off to the toilet."

I was incredulous, and I fear a little impatient, for I thought Janet was talking nonsense. "For heaven's sake, don't be silly! What made you think of that disgusting possibility?"

"Hand me that tin of lollies you were given this morning."

I got it for her and she looked at the back. "How many do you think he ate?" she asked.

"At least ten or maybe more," I told her; "in as many minutes too, or less. He was a real guts."

"Read what it says on the back of the tin."

I took the tin and read the small print: 'Sugarless. Restrict consumption to no more than five per day to avoid strong laxative effect.'

I stared at her. "How did you guess that?" I asked, utterly astonished.

"No guesswork," she assured me; "There had to be some reason for that outburst, and Horace is not mad. He probably thought he was about to pass a little wind – with embarrassing results. Sugarless sweets are inclined to have that effect. Horace Beetson's greed lost him that call."

I looked at Pauline and John. "Who says God doesn't answer prayers? Six months later the parish called a very fine and godly minister."

They were still laughing as they made their way out to their car.

Chapter 18

Oh what a tangled web . . .

A few days after John the Deacon's farewell, as we were sitting having breakfast one morning, Janet said "Mrs Jean McDonald has asked us out to dinner next Saturday evening. I've had a look at your diary and there's nothing there, so I accepted."

Jean was a crofter who lived on a croft with her son, some miles from the village. She was a widow, but her son helped her to run the croft. She was the epitome of kindness and generosity. She'd had a few problems she'd shared with me. They were not problems that I could do anything about on a practical level, but she'd asked me to uphold her in prayer which I assured her I would, and I did. Everything finally worked out well, and her life had taken a definite, upward turn.

"That's so kind of her," I replied. "I'll give her a call myself to thank her, and while I'm at it, I'll let her know that I'm a vegetarian, in case she isn't aware."

It was generally known around the congregation that I was a vegetarian, but I never assumed that everyone knew. Marilyn, whose son Alan had gone to live in Australia, certainly knew it. One day she gave me a fridge magnet, which claimed the word "Vegetarian" was a native American word meaning "lousy hunter." It sits proudly on our refrigerator door in Australia to this day.

Fowl, however, is a dish, in whatever form it is presented, that I have never been able to eat, even in my pre-vegetarian days. My sister, and one of our sons, are exactly the same. There is something about the smell of it that revolts me, let alone the taste.

I did ring Jean to thank her for inviting us, but true to form, forgot to mention the vegetarian message, and the following Saturday evening when amid a lot of happy conversation she brought in the steaming main dish, I suddenly remembered. The aroma of cooked chicken, so inviting to most, assailed my nostrils.

When Jean went out to fetch the carver, Janet whispered, "You know you're going to have to eat it, don't you? Mrs McDonald has gone to so much trouble, preparing this beautiful meal."

I gulped and nodded. I knew she was right. I'd have eaten it even if I'd been told it had hemlock sauce poured over it. I'm sure it was a lovely chicken dinner, for anyone who liked chicken. Janet certainly did, eating with every indication of enjoyment. I forced my large portion down without gagging, trying to show the same level of appreciation that Janet was showing. Jean was a wonderful hostess and it was a happy meal. I knew she would ask me later if I'd enjoyed the meal. I would not lie, but I had a plan...

One of my favourite people back in Australia was Arthur, a retired shearer who lived in Gunnedah. He once told me that when he went out to learn shearing as a young chap, there was no shearers' cook at that particular shed, so the old shearers decreed that the last one employed would have to take it on – which happened to be Arthur, who hated cooking. The rule was, if anyone complained about the food, the complainer had to take over as shearers' cook. Arthur was determined to get rid of the job. "The meals I dished up were vile," he told me, "but do you think I could get anyone to complain? Not a chance. They all bolted the meals down and had the hide to tell me how much they enjoyed my cooking. One day, I'd had enough. I went out into the paddocks and found some cow pats, which I took back to the cookhouse, threw them into the baking pans, threw in a bit of sauce and some vegetables, and baked this hideous concoction.

When the men came in for the evening meal, I served it up. The first man to try it took a mouthful, gagged, spat it out and bellowed, 'That's cow s**t – but beautifully cooked – beautifully cooked!'

"I was shearers' cook," Arthur concluded, "in that shed for the rest of the shearing season!"

I was ready when Jean posed the question, "How did you enjoy the chicken dish, Lachlan?"

"Jean, it was beautifully cooked – beautifully cooked! Thank you so much for going to so much trouble."

Janet too had a word. "It was a delicious meal, Jean- you're a marvellous cook."

Jean glowed. It was true – she was a superb cook.

Janet was also right of course, concerning the level of appreciation I should and did show, and on the way home we discussed it. "That meal was superb," she said; "I wish I could cook chicken like that."

"What am I going to tell her if she invites us out again?" I asked; "I can hardly tell her now that I'm a vegetarian."

The weeks slipped by, in which we were caught up in many parish activities and functions but one day Janet met me at the door after I'd been to the Dunbeath School.

"Guess what? Jean has invited us out again next Saturday. She's keen for us to go then because she's going to see family down in Ayrshire before going on a cruise and may not be back before we leave."

My heart sank. "Looks like there's a chance of another chook meal again. I hope I can force this one down."

"Well, as a matter of fact she did ask me what is your favourite dish, and I told her that Thai meal you always ask for when we eat out back in Australia. It's easy enough to prepare. She was really interested and told me she'd give it a whirl."

"You are indeed a wonderful wife," I told her, giving her a grateful peck on the cheek, "and worth every penny I don't pay you."

It was with a sense of relief and anticipation that we made our way out to the croft the following Saturday afternoon. Her son Ian was also present and entertained us, playing the pipes. "He's a member of the Halkirk pipe band," Jean told us proudly.

Finally we were ushered to the meal table. I felt Jean's eye upon me. "Janet told me you have a special favourite, Lachlan, and gave me the recipe. I hope you like it."

"I know I will, Jean – I've tried it before and I've also tried your cooking before. It has to be good."

Her hand was resting on the handle of the dish, ready to lift it. "You'll like it even better this time Lachlan. When I sampled what I'd cooked, I thought it was a little bland, so I added something I know you'll love!"

With a smile and a triumphant flourish she lifted the lid. She didn't have to tell me what she had added. I could smell it.

Chapter 19

The Flow Country

With the week closing, we decided to take Tuesday off as a rest day. Of course Janet had it all planned...

We drove off in the morning to Helmsdale, a village a few miles south of Lybster, marking the boundary between Caithness and Sutherland, where we had a relaxing coffee before heading north, surrounded by glorious scenery, up the strath of Kildonan.

As we travelled we were excited to have two encounters with wild deer; first in a heavily wooded area, and later as we drove by a great hill.

Deer, it seems to me, are bits of posers. On each occasion they paused long enough for me to get out the trusty camera and take a photo or three before dashing away with a toss of mighty antlers

We travelled through the picturesque and beautiful countryside, with the Helmsdale river rushing down one side, its banks dotted here and there with hopeful salmon fishermen.

Finally we arrived at the tiny hamlet of Forsinard which, surprisingly, has a tiny railway station where the train from Inverness to Thurso stops. Situated in the railway station building were a couple of rooms with a sign indicating they were for the use of the Forsinard Flows National Nature Reserve. In the rooms we found maps and brochures of the area.

The country around there is known as flow country – a vast area of bleak and apparently barren rolling peat moorlands.

As well, there are dubh lochans (dubh: Gaelic, meaning black. The peat turns the water dark). Lochans are small ponds. The dubh lochans dot the landscape.

The fragile peatlands are among the rarest in the world and are full of rare plant, bird and insect life. There is a guided four mile walk that one can do, but it was going to start a bit late for us, so we opted for a one mile walk on which we could take ourselves. We set off. Janet was reading up material and taking photos, peering down at little plants and things, while I was taking in the dramatic landscape out there, with its distant, beautiful hills and great skies. It is magnificent. It occurred to me that if one were lost out there in the middle of winter, it could prove seriously and even permanently fatal. It is so different from the rest of Caithness, but there is a lot of it out here, this flow country. It holds in balance a very special part of nature, and while we were there, we had a choir of many birds, chief among them the beautiful skylark.

Finally we left, and somewhere on the way home paused to enjoy the sandwiches and thermos of coffee Janet had brought. We sat, rapt in the beauty of the lonely hills. Turn off the car engine, and all one hears is the sigh of the wind...

Chapter 20

A classic mix-up

"I'm so excited, Lachlan!" Marilyn exclaimed for the sixth time as we sipped our tea.

She had asked me to drop in when I spoke to her after Church the previous Sunday.

As she ushered me down the rather narrow hall of her house I had to squeeze past a very large suitcase, so began to suspect Marilyn would be going away for few days.

As we had our tea she told me the reason for her excitement. "I'm going to Australia, Lachlan! I've mentioned my son over in Western Australia, haven't I?"

She had. Her son Alan, a heavy machinery operator, had gone for a holiday about five years previously, where he landed himself a very highly-paid job in the mines up north, and had stayed.

"It's my sixtieth birthday next week, Lachlan, so I'm going to pay him a surprise visit! He's often suggested I go over for a holiday, so now I'm going, but he has no idea!

I'm glad you called today, for I head off tomorrow."

It would be a long visit. "After all," she pointed out, "it's a long way, so it would be silly to go for a week."

A day later I saw Lybster's only taxi (apart from Addon's illegal one) heading towards the A99. Marilyn would be off to the airport at Wick, I surmised, probably to catch a plane to Glasgow, then another to Heathrow. Marilyn saw me and gave me an excited wave from the back seat of Lybster's lovely big white stretch limo. She was on her way to distant Australia.

The following morning I happened to be driving past Marilyn's house when I was surprised to see a stranger, loitering inside her gate.

"Hullo!" I thought to myself, "Don't tell me some shady character has found out Marilyn's away and is planning on breaking in."

I decided to investigate, so swung the car around and pulled up at Marilyn's gate.

The stranger emerged, looking a little preoccupied. He was about thirty years of age with a strong, weather-beaten face. He certainly didn't appear shifty – but, as I reminded myself, shifty people rarely do, and Addon was a good example.

"Can I help you?" I called.

He looked up and saw me. "I'm looking for Mrs Wilson," the stranger said. "I'm her son, Alan. I've just come from Australia. It's her birthday next week and I decided to pay her a surprise visit . . . is- is she all right?"

He must have seen my expression, for he paled. My hand had gone to my mouth and I was staring at him, horrified.

"Take a seat in the car," I said. "You aren't going to believe this!"

It was later, at the manse. I'd put his bags in the car and driven him up for a recuperative cup of tea.

"I can't believe it!" he'd said several times, shaking his head. "All the times I've asked her to come out and she decides to - at the very time I'm coming home! I'll have to catch the first plane I can back to Australia, and meet her there. She won't know where to go."

I went to the study and made a few urgent phone calls before hurrying back.

"Good news, Alan. If we can get you to Wick, there's a seat on a plane to Glasgow, leaving in about an hour. You'll arrive in Glasgow just in time to catch a plane to London. I've booked it for you. Pay when you get there. Use the phone here and try to get your return flight date altered. I'll book the taxi for you."

Alan altered his flight details. If he could get on the Wick and Glasgow flights, he was told, he would be able to catch his plane to Australia early tomorrow.

All the flight arrangements had swung smoothly into place.

We ran into a hurdle. The Lybster taxi was on a trip to Inverness. Time was running out. It was too late for a Wick taxi to come down and then get back in time.

I couldn't take him. As soon as I looked at the size of Alan's bag I knew it would never fit into the Golf, and there was other luggage as well.

"I swore I'd never, ever, have anything to do with Add-on John again," I said to Janet, "but this is an emergency. We may have to try for Addon's illegal taxi!"

I rang him.

"Certainly, Mr Ness." Addon assured me in his oily tone, "I can pick up the young man immediately. I'll get him to Wick airport in time."

"How much?"

"For you, £15.00."

"How much for him?" I asked suspiciously.

"The same," Addon replied, sounding a little hurt.

"Don't forget – it's a total of £15.00, Alan!" I told him as we hurried him and his bag to the manse gate; "Addon will take you down if he possibly can!"

"I know," Alan replied. "He was the village villain even when I lived here."

Addon's old illegal taxi, with Alan waving goodbye, disappeared in a haze of oily smoke towards the A99. Janet and I breathed a sigh of relief as we saw it turn right.

"Great news, Mr Ness!" It was Alan, calling from Glasgow. "I'm booked to leave here in about an hour. I'll stay at a pub overnight in London and fly out early in the morning, as I hoped. And there's even better news! The airline got in touch with my mother. She's half way to Singapore right now. She's decided to overnight there and wait for me, so we can fly to Australia together. Thank you for all your help!"

"Glad to be able to help, Alan. By the way, how did you get on with Addon John?"

"Great – he was great! When we got to Wick airport he helped me get my baggage to the terminal and then waited to make sure everything was OK."

"And all he charged was the £15.00?"

"Yes – oh, apart from the parking fee of course. He had to add £4.50 for the airport parking fee, so I gave him a fiver."

"I see," I said grimly. Wick is a small country town. There was no airport parking fee.

A couple of weeks later as I walked to the shops to buy 'The Bletherer" I was surprised to bump into Addon, who seemed in a hurry. Addon's normally regular features had been drastically if temporarily rearranged. Both eyes were blackened and his nose looked abnormally large and swollen.

"Hullo, Addon," I greeted him; "have you had an accident?"

"Walked into a door," the man mumbled through split lips before hurrying off. When he spoke I thought I detected a missing front tooth. I watched as he walked away. His gait appeared to be uncomfortable if not downright painful and I was reminded of someone I knew in Australia who'd been kicked by a horse. Maybe Addon was, among other thing, a horse trader...

Later, when I told Keith, the policeman nodded. "Aye – I had a word with him and he told me the same cock and bull story about walking into a door. I suspect 'the door' arrived in the form of the oil rig man who was ripped off by Addon, and who came back from Aberdeen to pay his old landlord a surprise visit. Addon didn't extend his 'holiday away' long enough and someone must have told the oil rig man he was back in town. Nothing can be proved of course, and Addon isn't saying anything, for obvious reasons. I think he thinks it's a case of least said, soonest mended".

Chapter 21

A fiery experience

"Lachlan," said Janet as we were getting into the car in front of the manse, "when you visit the hospital today, let me off at the gates and I'll walk down to the shops. Then I think we should have lunch. I'll meet you at McKay's Hotel."

We were on our way to Wick, where I planned to make my regular weekly visit around the patients at Wick hospital. It was an activity I quite enjoyed. I met many interesting people, and everyone seemed pleased to see me. I always made a point of wearing my clerical collar to the hospital, for it was a self-explanatory introduction, and when I spoke, the accent was immediately noticed. Most people were interested to know how I came to be in the far north of Scotland. I told them that we colonials are slowly drifting back to our roots. Some Australian ancestors were sent out in chains a couple of hundred years or so ago, while others were the victims of the Highland Clearances – not that I can claim any of either, as far as I know. These days in Australia it is quite fashionable to be able to claim as a forebear an early, unwilling settler who arrived in chains during the convict transportation days.

McKay's Hotel, almost opposite Wick hospital, is quite famous in the county of Caithness and even further afield. It is a fine hotel with an old world charm, and has an excellent cuisine. The hotel's main claim to fame however lies in the fact that it fronts the shortest street in the world: Ebenezer Place, which is exactly six feet, nine inches in length, or a little over a couple of metres. The front door of the hotel occupies about a third of the street. Janet and I had dined there a couple of times and John the deacon had taken us there as his guests to a Rotary Club dinner, where I was guest speaker.

Half an hour later, I was in the hospital, visiting the wards, stopping to chat with those I'd met previously, introducing myself to other patients and their visitors.

In one ward I saw a bed that had been curtained off but on the other side of the curtain I could hear the chatter of voices and an occasional laugh.

I found one of the nurses. "Would it be OK if I put my head around the curtain of that bed in the corner?" I whispered.

She smiled. "Certainly. That's Mr Drummond, a policeman. He's had an accident. The curtain's due to be removed anyway. It was put there when he had some pain medication."

The patient and visitors looked up as I stepped behind the curtain and threw them a smile.

"I hope I'm not intruding – just thought I'd say hullo. – I'm Lachlan Ness, the Latheron parish minister."

A middle-aged, fair-haired woman was seated by the bed, holding a hand of the patient, who was obviously her husband. His other hand lay on top of the blankets and was swathed in bandages. Standing on the other side of the bed was a large, somewhat overweight, police officer. His cap was set back on his head, revealing a shock of red hair. They all smiled, back, although the patient's smile was more a pain-filled grimace.

The police officer nodded a greeting. "Constable Tony Holmes, Reverend. Nice to see you."

The woman held out a hand. "I'm Julie Drummond, Mr Ness, and here in bed is my husband, Gordon, who's not sae well. He and Tony here had quite a nasty experience in the police car last night."

I turned to the patient. "Sorry to see you like this, Mr Drummond. I can see you're in real pain."

The man in the bed nodded ruefully. "Aye, you could say that, Reverend, but it was my ain fault – not one I'll make again, I can tell you that."

I opened my mouth to ask what happened, then closed it. Time has taught me to be discreet concerning a person's condition. It could be embarrassing. If Gordon Drummond wanted me to know, he'd tell me.

The patient must have noticed my hesitation. "You can ask me aboot it, Mr Ness, and I'll tell you, much as it embarrasses me to do so." He nodded towards the police officer.

"Tony and I were in the car last night, doing the rounds, when we came across some young kids, letting off fire crackers. We'd seen a rocket go up, which is what drew our attention.

Where the kids got them, I don't know and when we quizzed them, they wouldn't say. The kids were OK, and just handed us the crackers when we told them we were confiscating them.

On the way back to the station, I said to Tony, who was driving, 'I remember these things when I was a kid.' I don't know what got into me, but I pulled out my cigarette lighter, lit the fuse of one of the crackers and threw it out the window... well, I would have, if the window had been open! I'd opened it to chat to the kids and forgotten I'd closed it. The cracker bounced straight off the glass and fell into my lap. Before I could do anything, it went off. There was one helluva bang, the police car was full of smoke and fire and bits of red paper, and I'm screaming in pain. The cracker burnt the seat and door of the police car and put me in here." He held up his bandaged hand. "That happened when I tried to get the thing off my lap. Don't ask me about the damage down below though – it's too embarrassing."

As the patient told me the horrifying story, Constable Holmes, who must have heard it told countless times, started whistling softly. I recognised the tune but couldn't immediately place it.

Finally I took my leave and made my way across the road to McKay's Hotel, where I knew Janet would be waiting. The song Constable Tony Holmes had been whistling so softly kept running through my mind and I knew it would stay there until I remembered what it was.

The answer came to me just as I reached the door of the hotel. It was a song from the Musical, "Showboat: Smoke Gets In Your Eyes.

Chapter 22

An Oriental adventure

Janet was already seated in the dining room at MacKay's Hotel, when I walked in, and gave me a welcoming wave.

We had a look at the menu and were just considering ordering when we became aware of someone standing beside us. Glancing up, I was surprised to see an Oriental gentleman, about fifty years of age, small of stature and neat of appearance, obviously wanting to speak to me.

His dark eyes were friendly. "Excuse me for intruding," he began, bowing slightly, "I am Dr Toshi Turo, and I am here on behalf of my nephew and his wife at the table behind you. They and I would be most grateful if you would join us, as our guests."

We turned in our seats. Behind us were a young man and a woman, about thirty years of age, also Oriental, who were smiling in our direction, obviously waiting for us to respond.

Wondering what it was about, we prepared to stand. The man who'd spoken to us moved forward and courteously held Janet's chair as she arose, then led us to the other table.

The other couple stood as we approached. The younger man bowed a greeting and held out his hand, which I took.

"Thank you for agreeing to join us," he began. "I see that you are Christians, as are we – Japanese Christians. We have something we would like to discuss with you. My name is Sumio... Sumio Himura." He turned to the young woman. "And this is my wife, Nanako."

Nanako smiled at us. She was small, in the way of many Japanese women, and very attractive.

"I am very happy to meet you," she said, smiling demurely, and there was warmth in her dark almond eyes. Something about the way she spoke suggested it was a phrase she'd learned by rote. Her English, I suspected, was probably not fluent.

When we introduced ourselves, the two men looked amazed. "That accent!" exclaimed Dr Toshi. "You are New Zealanders? Australians?"

"Australians, "Janet said.

The two men looked at each other and grinned. "We have family members who live in Australia," said the younger man, "and we two have worked there from time to time in a professional capacity. It really is a pleasure to meet you, so far from home. What are you doing here?"

We told them. At first I'd wondered how Dr Toshi had known we were Christians, and then I remembered. The clerical collar was self-explanatory.

Sumio waved politely to the chairs. "Please, do sit down. We are honoured that you have agreed to be our guests."

I'd done a quick mental assessment. All three were impeccably dressed and obviously well-educated. The English of the two men was near perfect, and their manners excellent. It was plain that they were very familiar with Western ways.

A waiter took our orders and we turned our attention to our hosts.

"As I am sure you know, Mr and Mrs Ness," Sumio began, "there is a nuclear energy power plant at Dounreay, near Thurso that is currently being decommissioned. It will take many years to decommission it entirely, but my work there as a physicist is almost over. In a few weeks we, and my uncle Toshi, who also works at Dounreay as a scientist, will be returning to Japan. Before we do so, Nanako and I are hoping for a Christian blessing on our wedding. Would you consider doing that for us?"

"Aren't you already married?" I asked.

"Yes, last year, but it was what you would call a civil wedding, in Japan. Both Nanako and I feel our marriage will not be complete until it is blessed by God in a Christian ceremony."

"Well, I can't see why that would be a problem, Dr Himura, for as you're already married, it would simply be a wedding blessing."

Dr Himura looked relieved. "That is wonderful! By the way, I suggest we dispense with the formalities and use our Christian names."

The meals arrived, and over the food we discussed details of the service and where it would be held.

"I have a place in mind," Sumio said, "in a pretty park not far from Wick. If it rains, there is a nearby hall that I will book."

We set the date for a couple of weeks' time. "I'll need to visit you at home, so that we can discuss the service," I told them.

I had noted that Nanako had contributed almost nothing to the conversation. Sumio must have read my mind.

"Nanako does not have a great deal of English yet," he said, "but she is learning quickly. Uncle Tosh is teaching her – we call Toshi Tosh, by the way. He prefers it. He and I have worked on several projects around the world, so our English is very sound. In fact we are multi-lingual."

Sumio refused to let us pay for our meal, and when we left, with smiles all round, I'd made arrangements to visit the family at their home in a couple of days.

"What an amazing meeting!" Janet commented as we drove home, "and that's the first time we've met anyone who works at Dounreay."

We'd passed the nuclear energy power plant, visible from the road, a couple of times. To me, the unmistakable domes of nuclear plants always have a slightly sinister appearance, but now this one was being decommissioned as the Scots turned to exploring more sustainable, less dangerous forms of energy. There are hundreds of wind generators around Caithness, and wave energy is also being researched. The great North Sea greybeards that pound the rocky shores of Caithness may yet have a beneficial effect.

"I have heard," I said, "that there have been leakages of nuclear waste at Dounreay, and that the sea around there has been contaminated. It is illegal to fish within three miles offshore of the Dounreay plant. Fisherman who have done so, and eaten their catch, have been very visible at night – or so I'm told."

"How come?" Janet wanted to know.

"They glow green."

"Really?" replied my wife, amazed. Then she gave a disbelieving snort. "Rubbish!"

I smiled. Even after years of marriage, I can still reel her in occasionally...

A couple of days later, as arranged, I found my way to the Himura household, a unit in Wick, where the three lived.

Nanako answered the door and showed me into the lounge room. "Sumio and Uncle Tosh won't be rong," she said, in her quaint English; "they were derayed at the prant."

I noted that Nanako had not quite mastered the differences between English and Japanese, where 'L' becomes 'R' and vice-versa. She called me "Rachran" which from her sounded rather charming.

As we chatted I noted that the happiness I'd seen in her eyes previously now appeared to have gone, replaced by an underlying sadness.

"Nanako," I asked at last, "is everything OK?"

I could see that the question took her by surprise, and she was silent for a while before replying.

"Ah, Rachran, I am so sad. I do not think Sumio thinks I am pretty anymore." She pulled out a tissue and began dabbing her eyes.

"I find that very hard to believe, Nanako. What makes you think that?"

"Yesterday, we went out to dinner in the evening. Uncle Tosh and Sumio were ready before me. Sumio called out to me, 'Nanako – we are ready now. Put on your face and we will be on our way.' How could he tell me to put on my face? Does he not like the face I have?"

Despite myself, I gave a relieved laugh.

Nanako looked shocked. "Why do you raugh, Rachran?"

"Oh, Nanako, that is so funny! In the West, if a man tells a woman to 'put on her face,' or a woman says she is going to put on her face, it means putting on her make-up... you know, lipstick, eye shadow and all those things you girls use!"

Nanako's hand had gone to her mouth as she stared at me: "Leary?"

"Yes – really!" I replied, still laughing.

It was a different wife who greeted her husband and Uncle Tosh shortly after...

The three of us went through the order of service and at last we were all happy with it.

"I have a few words in Japanese you may like to learn, Lachlan," offered Uncle Tosh. "I've written them down on a sheet of paper. As well, I have a booklet of Japanese/English expressions you may care to look at. The service will be filmed of course, so that will be very nice for the families back in Japan."

"Do you want a hymn?" I asked, pocketing the paper and booklet. They'd arranged for a friend to play his keyboard at the service.

"Yes, prease!" said Nanako; "I'd rike 'Jesus Roves Me.' I know that one." So 'Jesus Loves Me' it was to be.

The day of the wedding blessing dawned bright and clear, despite a chilly little breeze that ensured coats and jackets would be worn in the pretty little park chosen for the service.

Sumio and Uncle Tosh had completed their contracts at Dounreay. After the wedding blessing the three would be on their way; a few days in London before flying back to Japan.

I'd carefully practised a number of the Japanese words and expressions from the suggestions and booklet that Uncle Tosh had given me and was fairly confident I had them off pat.

Because Nanako's parents were not able to be present, it had been arranged that I would escort Nanako down the 'aisle' to the small table, with its little brass cross, which would serve as a temporary altar. Janet and I had arrived early to set up the table.

A number of guests had started to arrive. Some of them were Japanese, and some of the Japanese women were wearing their colourful kimonos while others had settled for Western attire. Other guests, I suspected, were fellow workers from Dounreay.

Finally, Nanako arrived, looking stunningly beautiful in a dress of elegant pink with a matching shawl. When she stood beside me, I realised just how small and delicately framed she was. Janet helped her adjust her shawl. Finally, all was ready, and I gave the nod to the man on the keyboard. I could sense Nanako's nervousness.

"Oh, doki doki!" I whispered, ("Oh, how my heart beats!") and Nanako giggled as we set off...

The service went very well. I threw in a few Japanese words and made only one mistake. At the end, I smiled at the couple and said "Ohio Godzamous!"

Sumio and his bride stared back blankly.

Uncle Tosh, who was standing nearby, leaned over.

"You just said, 'Good morning!' he whispered. "Say, 'Omodetoh Godzamous' – congratulations!"

I did so, and everyone laughed.

After the hymn and the Benediction, we all milled and mixed, laughed and talked in the usual post-wedding euphoric way, but finally, it was time for Nanako and Sumio to leave. Tosh was their driver.

The wedding guests accompanied them to the car. Just as they were about to enter, I decided to air the final piece of Japanese that I had been practising.

I gave Nanako a farewell hug, shook hands with Sumio and Uncle Tosh and announced: "Saru Moh, keekera oshiru" which I thought was a form of blessing.

The three of them stared at me for a few moments before suddenly bursting into peals of laughter.

Uncle Tosh slapped his sides as the tears rolled down his face, and Sumio and Nanako had to hold on to each other. I could see that the other Japanese guests were similarly convulsed.

I sidled up to Uncle Tosh. "For Pete's sake, what did I say, Tosh?"

"You said," replied Uncle Tosh, then burst into laughter again... "You said, EVEN MONKEYS FALL OUT OF TREES!' Oh dear..." and again was overcome with mirth.

"Oh, Rachran, you are so fonnee," gasped Nanako at last; "we will never forget you, or your beautiful Janet!"

We watched the car out of sight. Somehow we knew we would miss them.

A couple of weeks later, the post lady delivered a parcel, all the way from Japan. When I opened it I found a very handsome fountain pen, with gold lettering on the side. There was a lovely little note from Sumio and Nanako, now happily settled back in their home in Japan.

We hope you like the pen, Lachlan, the note read. The gold lettering on the side is your name in Japanese. Uncle Tosh said to tell you that what you said as we were leaving is an old Japanese saying that means, 'anyone can make a mistake – even monkeys fall out of trees!' We know you did not mean that about our marriage! Now Nanako wants to finish.

There were a few kind words from Nanako and at the end she wrote, Uncle Tosh has taught me the proper use of L and R when speaking in English, but I would like to finish with something you will remember! With rots of rove flom us both!

"They sound so happy," Janet said with a sigh when we'd stopped laughing; "Nanako certainly has a great sense of humour."

I picked up the gift. "It's a 'Waterman' fountain pen," I said, examining it. "I wonder if I ever mentioned that I like to collect fountain pens, especially Watermans? I don't think so. Anyway, this is quite an expensive one, and I'll treasure it – it will always remind us of them."

Chapter 23

The Western Highlands

A couple of weeks earlier, Janet had said to me "Lachlan, you've been really busy for quite some time now. It's time you took a couple of days off so that we can do some exploring. It would be a shame if we came all this way, and saw only this part of Scotland, lovely as it is. Let's go away, for a couple of days at least."

I knew it was sound advice. I (like many of my colleagues in my own and doubtless other denominations who had 'put their hand to the plough and not looked back') am not good at taking time off. Had it been up to me, I would probably have been content to remain in the parish and simply work. Janet does not think like that. She wanted to see some more of Scotland beyond the boundaries of our beautiful parish.

We agreed to take a couple of days away.

One Sunday following the morning services and a quick lunch, we were on the road.

We headed north-west to Thurso, just twenty-five miles away, right on the very top of mainland Scotland, then west, into the neighbouring county of Sutherland, which goes all the way to the west coast and the mighty mountains of the Western Highlands.

We paused briefly at the village of Melvich, then Betty Hill, where we found a small roadside cafe and enjoyed a break and a coffee. There was a graphic warning on a sign we saw at Strathy Point: Please do not take your dog beyond this point. The cliffs are unfenced and sheep are liable to panic and go over the edge.

As we travelled, the country became increasingly mountainous, wild, lonely and extraordinarily beautiful – and we had travelled only fifty miles or so from the gentle green hills of Caithness!

The road was single track – that is, one car wide, with passing places here and there to duck into when one meets a car coming the other way.

I had to stop every half mile or so to photograph some new and beautiful scenery; seeing in the misty distance the majestic, castellated shape of Ben Loyal towering above all the others.

Finally we arrived in the pretty township of Tongue, or in the Gaelic, Tunga. Tongue rests in the shadow of Ben Loyal.

We drove ever onwards, heading west, and I was 'minded of the lovely Scottish song, "Westering Home."

We passed down the lovely waterway of the Kyle of Tongue until we reached the tranquil waters of Loch Eriboll. It is a massive sea loch. During WW2 it was a mustering point for convoys. We read that the sailors used to call Loch Eriboll "Loch 'orrible,"– probably because they were there during wild winter storms and blizzards.

We travelled on and on, stopping often for photos. We came to one pleasant place and pulled over to take a few photos.

As I stood, I heard a lamb calling from a nearby hill. I strained my eyes, but just could not pick it out. The baahing seemed to be coming from exactly the same spot and went on and on.

Finally, curiosity overcame me, so I followed the sound up the hill. Half way up, there was a fault that formed a narrow dirt path along the grassy hill. Erosion had formed little hollows, like mini-caves – and it was in one of them that I found my lamb. The little fellow had backed into one of the mini dirt caves for reason or reasons unknown, but when he tried to leave, his shoulders were just too wide. All that was poking out were his neck and head, from which peered a couple of anxious eyes. I reached down, grabbed him by his woolly shoulders and gave a sharp tug. At once the cave's dirt sides crumbled and broke off and the little chap was free. He went charging off down the hill without even a grateful bah, to be reunited with his relieved mother. How long he had been stuck there I could not guess, but not too long, for he was in good nick. After I had done all that, I kicked myself for not taking one photo.

Finally, roughly one hundred miles from Lybster, we arrived at the town of Durness, where we intended to stay the night.

Durness is the most north-westerly town on the Scottish mainland. Cape Wrath, the most westerly point of mainland Scotland, is about ten miles further west, but the day was cold and overcast with a mist, so we decided not to go. We would have had to depend on a ferry anyway, for some of the trip.

There are only a few small shops but lots of B&Bs in Durness. Most of them had "No Vacancy" signs, but we saw an old place with a free room, so booked in.

We were shown into a tired old room with three single beds and a bit of ancient furniture in it, but it looked comfy enough, and indeed the beds were very comfortable. Also in its favour was the price, which was considerably cheaper than most B&B's, so we had a good deal.

We were not much further north than Lybster but a long way west. It was still broad daylight, so we went to explore the famous "Smoo Caves." The caves are situated at the foot of a cliff on the edge of the town. They were inhabited in Viking and earlier times by fishermen. The word "Smoo" is from the Norse Smuga, or cave, and there is a similar Gaelic word for cave: smudha. We had a good look through them.

After an excellent breakfast the following morning, we had a good look around Durness, including the pretty Bay of Balnakiel, accessed via a narrow road with stone walls either side.

Finally we drove on, heading south towards Lairg, down by the Kyle of Durness, with the great mountains towering around us as we drove by majestic Highland hills. It is hard to describe it all. Remoteness, isolation, beauty, grandeur, tumble as descriptions through one's mind, but there is even more; a sort of elusive spiritual quality that defies accurate description. I would use 'awesome" if it were not so trite from over-use these days. All the same, we were filled with a sense of awe, in the spiritual sense, as in Psalm 121.

On we drove down that narrow, narrow road, past the mighty Ben Ghlas, heading south.

By the shores of serene Loch Inchard we found a lonely hotel: hotel Richonich. It was a very appealing in appearance, so we decided to stop for morning tea. From its window we looked down the long loch with its looming hills.

It was a journey of seemingly never-ending lochs, burns and great mountains. On the way we were thrilled to see the heather starting to bloom on the hills, which had not happened yet in Caithness, but by then we would have been well south of Lybster.

We were amazed at the difference between the east and west coasts, only a hundred miles apart. Caithness is mainly gentler green hills and glens, while the west of Sutherland inspires awe and amazement – especially for us Australians.

Finally, vast Loch Shin came into view across the misty hills. We travelled down and down, with glorious views across its waters, until we reached our next main town: Lairg.

Lairg had the feel of a well-heeled, prosperous sort of a town - reinforced when we discovered that there is a branch of the famous HARRODS there!

First, however, we travelled a bit out of town to see the famous Shin falls, where at that time of the year the salmon jump on their journey to their spawning place.

We found the falls, which are not wildly spectacular, but were thrilled indeed to see leaping salmon! Unfortunately, every time I clicked the camera, I was a tad too late and all I was left with were some good shots of white water.

We found the attractive Harrods shop, and entered, Janet uttering little yelps of excitement as she hurried in, tail wagging. Near the entrance there was a life-sized figure of what we took to be Harrods owner, beaming down upon us, kitted out smartly in Highland dress.

As we ate a bowl of very tasty soup with a roll for a very late lunch, I remarked, "This morning we were breakfasting in possibly one of the less exotic establishments in the Western Highlands. This afternoon we are dining in one of the most exotic!"

Our arrival at Lairg coincided with the arrival of heavy rain, so we did not stay too long. Finally, we headed eastwards to the fair township of Colspie, which is the home of majestic Dunrobin Castle. "I've heard so much about Dunrobin Castle," Janet remarked. I hope we can fit in a visit one day."

We did not linger there however, but headed back to the far north, and the gentle highland hills of Caithness; back tae hame and hearth.

Chapter 24

The Bickerings

I had asked the Latheron parish folk some time before to write down for me people who, they thought, were in need of a visit. Everyone was quite helpful and I had enough names in a very short time to last me for many weeks. As I examined the list, one name in particular caught my eye: Mr and Mrs Bickering. What an unusual name, I thought, but in the long list of unusual surnames around the world, Bickering would hardly rate a mention. All the same, I decided to check first with Pauline the session clerk, and when I showed it to her, she laughed. "They're not on our parish roll, Lach. In fact I think they're C of E, but there's no Church of England around here so occasionally they come to our church. Someone must have thought it would be nice for you to drop in on them. As well, that's not their real name, but I wouldn't be surprised if some think it is though, for they've been called that for years. Their real name is Bert and Gertrude Smithers, but of course they get Bertie and Gertie. They're English, but they've lived up here for years. I'd better give you a bit of background information. First, they've been away. I believe there was a family tragedy down in England. They're a very nice couple, and very agreeable to talk to – but not when they're talking to each other! They're always bickering over nothing, which of course is how they got their nickname. If one says something's black, the other will swear it's white. The amazing thing is, they really are fond of each other, and it's only a bit of a game – well, that's what most folk around here think. They're both on the stout side. I was chatting to the doctor one day after he'd been out to see them. Gertie wasn't well, and was confined to her bed. He examined her and told her to roll on her left side. 'But doctor,' she said, 'I don't have a left or right side – as you can see, I'm perfectly round!' The doctor was very amused!"

"I'm amused too, Pauline," I said. "I hope I can meet them. They sound quite funny."

"I hope you meet them too, Lach. They live quite a way out, down a rather remote little lane. Finding their house is a bit on the tricky side."

The following day I happened to drop in on Robert, one of the elders. "A visit you should make soon, Lachlan," said Robert, "is to see Wullie. He's an old soldier and none too well. I think he'd like to see you. He knows his Bible back to front, but he can't get to church any more. By the way, he has only one leg. He'll tell you about it."

Most folk baptised William around those parts are rarely called that name. Most are known as Wullie, or Willie.

Wullie, Robert continued, had been a pre-World War 2 career soldier, and by the outbreak of hostilities was a Regimental Sergeant Major (RSM). I learned that he proudly served in the Black Watch Regiment and remained in the Army until retirement.

Robert had given me sound directions to Wullie's place, but there were some funny little side roads around the district that meandered off into nowhere in particular, and it was not hard to lose one's way. I enjoyed drives down some of those hidden roads, for sometimes they led to lovely out of the way places that we would not have encountered otherwise.

Somehow, on the way to Wullie's hoose, I missed a turn or two and found myself driving down a winding lane that I'd had no idea was there. Peaceful green fields with grazing sheep were on either side, but ahead was a house tucked away by itself. It was time to ask directions, so I pulled into the drive. My knock on the door was greeted by frenzied barking from what sounded like multiple dogs, for I detected the deep bark of a large dog while the other had an unmistakable yappy sound to it. 'Either I'm listening to a dog with an identity problem,' I told myself, 'or there are at least two dogs in there.' I hoped that the householders were in, for I always enjoyed meeting both people and their animals. Anyway, I went on to explain to myself, I expected to be there only long enough to ask directions . . .

I'd been right about the dogs As the door opened, two dogs rushed out and began to spring about me, still barking excitedly, but they were unmistakably welcoming barks. One was a German short-haired pointer and the other a little Skye terrier. I looked up to see a man, small and round and balding, standing in the doorway. "Can I help you?" he asked.

"I love your dogs!" I greeted him, bending to pat them; "I'm looking for Wullie's house, but I've missed a turn somewhere. Would you know where he lives?"

As soon as I started to speak, the other's face lit up. "You must be the Australian minister we've heard about!" He held out his hand, which I took. "G'die, mite! That's the way you Australians speak, isn't it? My name's Bertie - Bertie Smithers. Come in – I know Gertie's been looking forward to meeting you." As the words tumbled out I realised that, completely unawares, I had found my way to the house of the so-called Bickerings.

We made our way down the hall, accompanied by the still-barking dogs. The sound was deafening in the restricted space of the hall, but Bertie didn't seem to notice. He simply raised his voice. "You can probably tell that I'm not Scottish. Neither's Gertie. We're Geordies but we love it up here…"

Bertie ushered me into the sitting room, just as his wife walked in – I was sure it was Bertie's wife, for she was about the same age and generous proportions as Bertie. As Pauline had indicated, she could be described as 'robust – more bust than ro,' as I'd once heard someone else described.

"Lachlan," said Bertie, "I'd like you to meet my wife. Gertie, meet Lachlan, the Aussie minister we've heard about. I told him you'd like to meet him."

Gertie's face broke into a welcoming smile. "That's marvellous! We've heard you were visiting around the district, Lachlan, and hoped you'd get to see us. You and Bertie sit down and I'll make the tea."

She hurried off and we sat. The big dog came forward and put his head on my knee, gazing up at me with sad brown eyes, while the little one hopped up on the lounge beside me for a closer inspection, so I patted each in turn.

Bertie watched approvingly, obviously pleased that I was at ease with his two dogs. "The big dog's name, is Albert," he said. "He's a German short-haired pointer so we named him after Queen Victoria's hubby, who was German, and the little one is a Skye terrier, so we called her Victoria, or Vicky for short. Queen Victoria loved Scotland and was often at Balmoral castle."

I smiled as I patted the dogs. "They're lovely-natured dogs Bertie, and I'm sure Queen Victoria would have approved."

Just then Gertie bustled in with tea, biscuits and cakes. "We're so thrilled you managed to visit. We're Church of England – what they call Episcopalian in Scotland. There's no Episcopalian church up here, so we sometimes go down to Inverness. We sing in the choir when we can get there."

"I believe you've had a family bereavement," I said. "Pauline told me."

"It was terrible, Lachlan! My cousin Freda who was about my age, topped herself – you know – committed suicide. We couldn't believe it, could we Bertie?"

"Well… Bertie began, with what I assumed would be a qualifying remark, but Gertie hurried on: "I mean, she didn't have any reason to do it – none that we've been able to figure out. When I got the news on the phone I went the colour of chalk and had to sit down for about –"

"What colour?" interrupted Bert.

"What do you mean?" snapped Gertie, obviously annoyed at being interrupted.

"You said you went the colour of chalk! What colour did you go? There's red chalk, blue chalk, yellow chalk –"

"White chalk, you idiot!" snapped Gertie again; "What colour do you think?"

Bert didn't respond, so Gertie continued her story: "Freda left a note and in it said she wanted that hymn, Immortal, invisible played in the service. It has one of the prettiest tunes, called Joanna --"

"The tune's called St Denio," broke in Bertie.

"It's Joanna, Bertie!"

Bertie opened his mouth to speak. I cleared my throat. They looked at me.

"You're both right," I told them. "I love that hymn too. In some hymn books the tune is called Joanna and others, St Denio."

They both said "Oh!" together, and were quiet for a time. Then Gertie continued her sad story in detail, but at last it was over. "There's a photo of Freda somewhere – you'll see what a lovely person she was. I was looking at it the other day after we got back from the funeral, but I can't think where I put it."

"You put it in our bedroom, dear," Bert reminded her; "in the second drawer of the chest of drawers."

"You mean the middle drawer."

"The second drawer is the middle drawer!"

"From what end?

"From either end, you idiot!" There was growing exasperation in Bertie's voice.

It began to dawn on me just how accurate was the 'bickering' description, but I could detect no feeling of rancour; in fact they appeared to be enjoying themselves. I had the strangest feeling of being the sole viewer of a funny comedy.

Finally, I got up to go. "Thank you both for a most entertaining couple of hours. I hope we can meet again. Can you tell me how to get to Wullie's house?"

Gertie answered first. "Drive to the end of this lane and turn right," she told me, holding out her left arm, "and then . . ."

"Don't be daft, Gertie!" interrupted her husband, holding up his right arm; "drive to the end of the lane and turn left."

It was some time before I managed to get away, but I was still chuckling, telling myself that I must bring Janet to meet them. I knew she too would be made just as welcome. I wanted her to meet those marvellous folk, and the dogs, and enjoy their company as I had. As I drove, I pondered the question of accents, and how Australiana apparently sound to non-Australians, and Bertie's crack about "G'die, mite!" That was the second time I'd heard that. John the deacon had joked of it when he'd introduced us to his adorable border collie, Meg. Someone else I'd met said that for a long time, he thought Australians came from a strange place called "Estraya" which is the way some Australians apparently pronounce "Australia." Then again, I remembered being told by an English rector of an Australian Anglican church that in England his church choir, when singing the hymn "Praise My Soul, the King of Heaven" sang the line, "Praise Him for His grace and favour" as "Preese Him for His grease and fever" while his Australian church choir sang it as "Prise Him for His grice and fiver." Accents... they change meanings. In one parish in Australia, many years ago, a new family arrived from Scotland. After they introduced themselves to me, I introduced them to the congregation as "Mr and Mrs Teeler and family." It turned out that their name was not Teeler, as I'd heard, but "Taylor." Then again, what about the folk across the Tasman in New Zealand, who pronounce 'i' as 'u' and 'e' as 'i'...? Lost in my thoughts and reminiscences, I only just avoided ending up in a ditch...

Meanwhile, I knew I would have to ask someone else for directions to Wullie's place...

Chapter 25

Wullie

After a further enquiry I finally found Wullie's house, no more than a ten-minute drive from the Bickerings.

When I knocked on Wullie's door I could hear the measured sound of his crutch on the wooden floor as he approached. The door opened to reveal a tall, straight-backed man with thinning hair. His bearing and manner had "soldier" written all over him, despite the crutch, for his left leg was gone just above the knee. I'd seen many proud old soldiers like Wullie over the years. I'd have put him well into his eighties.

"Welcome to my wee bothy, Lachlan," he said as he held open the door after I'd introduced myself. I'd already come across the word 'bothy' which was a Caithness word, usually referring to something like a rough hut or temporary shelter, or even a hut on a farm for a farm worker. I'd asked someone when I'd noted that there is a fishermen's bothy in Dunbeath. In the old days, I was told, it was used for fishermen about to set out to or return from a night's fishing. Wullie's was no bothy but a comfortable little cottage.

The old man led me through to a small but comfortable parlour and motioned me to sit. I watched him as he carefully lowered himself into a chair. "I have tae be a wee bit carefu' these days, Lachlan," he said when he was comfortable, "for the older I get, the harder it is to get oot of a chair again."

"It must be even more difficult, trying to manage on one leg," I replied.

"Aye, it is indeed, but I'm used to it and it was nae good even before they took it off doon at Fraserburgh many years ago. It was an old war injury that became worse as time went on, and finally the doc said either it went, or I would, so I had little choice. It still pains, you mind, but I find a dram or two of whisky a day helps a lot… in me, of course – not on the leg! All the same, when I go, we'll be reunited, that leg and I, because I brought it back up here tae Caithness with me. It's doon noo, in the grave where one day I'll be buried."

The old man must have seen my surprised expression. He smiled.

"I see you're a wee bit surprised, Lachlan, but don't worry – you're no' the furrst. It's a matter of faith, y'see. When the Lord returns in glory, and the graves give up their dead, there is no way I want tae be hoppin' all the way back tae Aberdeenshire on one leg tae fetch the one they took off, so I brought it back wi' me…"

I waited, fascinated, to hear the rest of the story, but we were interrupted by a knock on the door, and Wullie went off the answer it. I could hear footsteps returning, and voices, before Wullie ushered in his next visitor. "No, no, Dr Burt," he was saying, "it's nae a problem. Come in, come in…"

Dr Burt was a fair-haired, middle-aged man, known in the district to be very competent. Janet and I had been to see him professionally, and were impressed by his thoroughness and friendliness.

His wife and young family were regular attenders at the Lybster congregation. "I'm sorry I'm not more regular at the Kirk, Lachlan," the doctor had once said to me when I'd visited their home, "but somehow I always seem to be on duty on Sundays" and it was a fact - Dr Burt was a hard working, fine doctor.

I stood to leave as the doctor entered. "I don't mind if the minister stays," said Wullie; "in fact I'd prefer it."

The doctor looked at him. "Are you sure, Wullie?"

"Aye, I'm sure right enough."

I sat in the corner while the doctor ran an expert eye over his patient. He was very thorough. Finally, he put away his stethoscope. "I know it's for your pain, but how much are you drinking these days Wullie?"

The old man thought for a moment. "Och, not a great deal, doctor; just a dram here and there, ye mind."

"And how often is your 'here and there' Wullie?"

Wullie shifted uncomfortably in his seat. "Nae sae often – and it's just a wee dram, y'ken."

"And just how wee is your 'wee dram,' Wullie?" pursued the doctor.

Wullie squirmed and wriggled, but the doctor would not let him off the hook, and finally it emerged that Wullie was drinking far too much.

"You'll have to cut it down, Wullie," the doctor said as he departed, "or it'll be the death of you!"

"Ah well," Wullie said after the doctor had gone, "I'm not planning on living tae be a hundred anyway!" It was obvious the old man didn't want to pursue the story of his leg, so I didn't pursue it.

The old soldier had a wonderfully independent spirit and scorned help, insisting on living "all alane" in his wee bothy, as he called it.

Wullie was delighted to learn that I had about sixteen years' service as an Australian Regular Army chaplain and from then on I was referred to as "padre." As we sat and chatted he told me of all the fine old padres, of many different denominations, he'd known during his years in the Army.

Over the next few weeks, during my regular visits, he spoke a lot about the war. "I know you Aussies think ye beat the Germans single-handed at El Alamein," Wullie used to say with a chuckle, "but it's no' the way it was. A lot of us Brits were there too, including me, and we were at Gallipoli too, in the First World War. We did our bit.

O' course, if it wasnae for John Wayne, Jerry would have won, hands doon. Och – that man was amazing – he fought and won on land, sea and in the air. No wonder Jerry didnae stand a chance!"

Wullie was interested to learn that my uncle Tom, a Scot who was my mother's brother, had also fought at Cape Helles, Gallipoli, in the Highland Light Infantry.

When I called, I generally found him pottering about in his superb garden, back as straight as a ramrod, his flowers obediently standing to attention in perfectly straight rows. It occurred to me sometimes that at Wullie's command they would have marched smartly off.

One day Wullie had a nasty fall while cleaning out a drain, and at his age, frail and with old war injuries still affecting his ailing frame, the prospects were not good.

I arrived at the hospital at the same time as his brother, Ewen. Wullie was behind a closed curtain, being tidied up by a nurse. "Dear me, Wullie," we could hear her say, "just look at you! You're a' boorach!

We cannae have you greeting your friends and relations like this!" She came out from behind the curtain, gave us a brief smile and went off to get something for Wullie.

"What's 'boorach' mean, Ewen?" I asked.

"It's a Caithness word," Ewen explained. "It simply means 'messy' or even 'dirty.'"

The brothers were close, and Ewen often popped in at Wullie's hoose, where I'd met him. He was somewhat smaller and younger than his brother, and was now deeply troubled.

When the curtain was removed, Ewen sat by his brother and took his hand. "Ah, Wullie, Wullie, ye auld fool ye – diggin' in a ditch at your age!" He shook his head sorrowfully. "Hitler couldnae kill ye, Wullie, despite trying, but I fear ye may ha' done it tae yersel' this time!"

The old soldier turned to me. I had to bend closer to hear him. "Aye, it could be true, padre. I have a feeling that the CO, the Captain of all our souls, may be posting me to higher duties at Command HQ..."

Chapter 26

Wullie's funeral

The call we were half-expecting came next morning. Wullie had heard the CO's posting order, and obeyed.

I was saddened to learn the news. I had grown fond of the old soldier.

I went to visit some of Wullie's extended family (he was an old bachelor), and to offer help with the general arrangements. The funeral was set for the following Thursday.

On Thursday morning we gathered in one of the small churches in the parish, to reunite Wullie with his physical leg and his soul with the Lord in Whom he trusted. The sky was dismal, and shed a few tears.

After the brief service in the Kirk, the cortege moved slowly off to the cemetery which, like many of the cemeteries in Caithness, has glorious views over the sea.

The weather was, to say the least, inclement. We walked down the hill to the graveside and stood with a cold strong wind tearing at us, as a huge black cloud hovered above, ready at any moment to unload another torrent of the sort that had descended on the Kirk just a short time before, during the service.

There was almost a dreamlike quality about the funeral... the massive, dark cloud above us, the small band of black-clad mourners huddled around the open grave, my black gown fluttering and whipping in the wind. Before us the cold grey circle of the North Sea swept onto the dramatic sea-cliffs of Caithness, while behind us stood lonely green hills, misted with rain – so different from what I'd known.

Suddenly I was no longer in Caithness. A memory, almost as vivid as the occasion itself, flashed into my mind – a memory of many years ago. I was standing again in a cemetery on the edge of a small village that struggled for existence on the hot dry plains of western New South Wales. Beside me stood the two sons of the deceased grazier – killed when his horse rolled on him. They had dug their father's grave, six feet down into solid black soil, in the paddock that constituted the town cemetery. In the distance we could see a cloud of dust, signalling the approaching hearse, seemingly travelling several feet above the road, riding a heat haze. The hearse came down from Walgett town; an ancient Studebaker, 1940 vintage. It arrived beside us, the dust billowing around it before rolling over us. The undertaker wore a pin-striped suit, probably around the same vintage as the hearse. He had on a crumpled checked shirt, held together at the top by a grubby red tie. The graveside service was short. The heat saw to that…

I felt myself being nudged back into Caithness: "We're ready to lower the coffin, Mr Ness," the funeral director whispered.

To be asked to be a pall-bearer is considered a special privilege in many parts of Scotland. There is a tradition, lowering the coffin on its silken cords.

The funeral director called out the number… "One!" and the person allocated the first cord stepped forward to take it; then two! And so on.

It was taking time, and I kept glancing apprehensively above at that mighty cloud, taunting us with a few cold sprinkles. The funeral director, mind fixed firmly on the solemnity of the occasion, cared not a whit for anything but the task at hand, 'come wind, come weather.'

All the eight bearers held a cord each side of the coffin, and at the undertaker's word, the coffin was lowered slowly into the rich dark earth. The coffin in place, the undertaker called for the cord holders to let the cords go as one, and they fell with a muffled thud onto the coffin: "Earth to earth… ashes to ashes… dust to dust…" During the committal, as I mentioned each, the undertaker reverently threw some earth into the grave.

There was no bugler but the funeral director had a recording. We stood to attention as "Last Post" followed by "Reveille" rose into the air to meet the sky…

Finally, it was all over:

Soldier, rest! Thy warfare o'er...

(Sir Walter Scott: "The Lady of the Lake").

We made our way slowly back to our vehicles, the sad funeral aura hanging like a cloud over us. The watery cloud above still hung off.

The moment we were all in our vehicles, down it came – a veritable wall of water. I thanked God for letting us get the committal over before that cloud burst its watery sides.

We gathered in the home of one of Wullie's relatives for a cup of tea before I drove home – and was saturated getting from the car into the manse.

A couple of days later, when I walked into the manse after doing some visiting I found Janet poring over a map.

"Lachlan, do you realise we have been here all this time and haven't yet managed to get down to Inverness? I think on our next day off we should go – and while we are there, do one of those cruises on Loch Ness!"

Chapter 27

Loch Ness

The following Monday (Monday was our usual day off) we were on the bus to Inverness.

On the way south we were amazed at the depth of green of the countryside, which almost defies description. Even the leaves of the trees were the lushest and greenest one could possibly imagine. It was good to be able to sit in the bus and see it without having to worry about the driving. We had a good trip down and then a good look about that old-world town of Inverness. It is called 'the capital of the northern highlands' for there is no other place anything like as big.

We had lunch before taking another bus that delivered us a short distance to the jetty at the Caledonian Canal, where we and a large crowd of fellow tourists boarded a ferry called "Jacobite Queen."

Soon we were headed down the lovely Caledonian Canal, on our way to the Loch.

At last we saw the great waters of Loch Ness stretching away before us. The scenery was breathtaking, with the great mountains surrounding the waters before marching away into the distance. The day itself added to the dramatic effect, for there was a lot of cloud about, and rain and mist. The waters are always very dark, because the water rushing from the great hills is affected by the peat. It is a mysterious loch, for it is astonishingly deep, at 750 feet. That's about 230 metres.

Did we see Nessie? No, I am very sorry to say we did not, but my camera was poised every inch of the way.

Is there a "monster" in Loch Ness? I believe so. I have always believed it and sightings go back to St Columba in the 5th century AD. Too many good, reliable people have claimed to have seen it and wait – there's more.

On the way to the ferry, the bus driver showed us a clipping from the local paper of the previous month. The boat on which we were due to travel had recorded an object it had picked up 64 feet under the keel of the boat. It was the largest object ever recorded on a sonar in Loch Ness, and it was moving (that is, swimming), 64 feet down there, in those dark waters. The photo of the sonar reading was in the local paper. The boat's crew were all a bit coy and would not say unequivocally that it was Nessie; they simply showed what the sonar reading was, and we could make what we like of it, we were told.

We made our way down to the ancient 14th century ruin of Urquhart Castle and stayed there quite a while, exploring it and reading its ancient history.

Finally a bus collected us and delivered us to Inverness where we boarded our bus to the north, and home.

It had been quite a day.

The next day I visited Margaret Gunn, and with Red the black and white cat purring contentedly on my knee, told her the Loch Ness story.

Margaret listened closely. "That's a most interesting story, Lachlan. I've always believed there is something very unusual in the loch, and like you, can't believe everyone who has claimed to have seen Nessie is a hoaxer, a liar, or has simply mistaken a floating log for the creature. It's worth searching for something substantial among all the red herrings. In fact," she continued, "I have a story of my own – not that I have seen the creature, you mind. Years ago, I visited an abbey, situated on the shores of Loch Ness which, sadly, is not there now. One of the monks told me he had definitely seen 'Nessie.' He said the creature was quite visible, and he watched it for some time. In fact he said he was incapable of moving! Finally, it disappeared. Highly excited, he ran to tell the prior, the head of the abbey, who said, 'Unless I see it with my own eyes, I will not believe it!' It reminded me of a similar response that can be found in John chapter 20:24-30."

I nodded. "Yes – it's a pity people can so easily dismiss something others have seen or heard, simply because what they've been told is outside their own experience. It's rather a blinkered way to look at life. I'd hate to be a perpetual Doubting Thomas."

I took a closer look at Margaret. Her face was pale, and I suspected she was in pain.

"Margaret – you don't look well. Can I get you something? Would you like me to call the doctor?"

She smiled wanly. "Thank you, Lachlan – no, I've medication I can take for the pain, but finally, there's nothing anyone can do anyway."

It was the first time she's made any reference to her terminal illness. She'd not missed church, and always seemed cheerful, brushing off any query made regarding her health. I felt a stab of sorrow. Janet and I had grown very fond of Margaret.

Chapter 28

The death of Margaret Gunn

Since Eileen in the shop had told us about Margaret Gunn and her failing health, I had made a point of regularly visiting her.

Her great yet simple faith, and her natural goodness, made her a pleasure to be with. As well, I loved her cats.

During my visits we sat each side of her cosy fire, with her cats draped comfortably on various chairs – big Red, the black and white cat, usually on my lap – and discuss all manner of things. Margaret had a very keen mind and was well-read theologically. Her faith was inspirational. I'd learned that she'd lived all her life in Lybster, apart from time away at University before returning to teach at Wick

She grew up in The Ha' (which colonials would not be able to pronounce properly, the locals had assured me – and they were right). It means "The Hall" as in "Toad Hall" and is now called "Lybster House." It dates back to the 17th century; a grand old residence, now invisible behind a lovely wooded garden across the field from the manse.

People in the village and in the church had told me of Margaret's indomitable spirit, and her gifts in art and music.

"Aye, she's a wonderful person," Eileen told me once, "and very gifted – not that you'd ever learn that from her. She has the funniest sense of humour! She inherited her love of art and music from her mother, but her sense of fun from her father."

As the weeks passed, I could see that Margaret was getting frailer, but she never spoke of it, so I never mentioned it.

Each Sunday I looked for Margaret, sitting at her favourite place in the Church – but one day she wasn't there.

"She's been taken to hospital in Wick," Pauline the session clerk told me, "late last night."

From then on I visited her often. She had many visitors.

Not long after she was admitted, Janet and I went in to see her. I had a block of nutmilk chocolate, my favourite, for her.

"I hope you're a chocoholic, like me, Margaret," I told her, "but if you're not, I'll take care of this for you."

She smiled. "Sorry, Lachlan – I'd love to have some, but that is one of the things I'm not permitted now, but nutmilk was always my favourite."

"Oh well, it's an ill wind, and all that," I answered jovially. "I'll tell you what, Margaret – I'll bring you in a chocolate each time, but as you can't have any, I'll eat it myself and think of you. How does that sound?"

She laughed. "I'm sure I'll enjoy them by proxy, Lachlan!"

On the way out, Janet said, "Lachlan – you are so awful! That's what you did to George – and he loves chocolate. All you ever took him when he was in hospital was the empty wrapping each time, to prove you'd had good intentions – you had the gall to eat them on the way in!" Our friend George knew only too well what it was, to have a cunning and devious chocoholic for a friend…

A month later, as I sat by Margaret's hospital bed, it was obvious the end was very near. She knew she was dying – had known for months. We shared a final prayer and the Benediction. I could only just manage it.

As I rose to leave, Margaret reached out a slender white hand. "Lachlan," she whispered, "I feel like some nutmilk chocolate. Would you have some, for me?"

She smiled her lovely smile and closed her eyes.

She died that night.

The following Tuesday afternoon, after a service at the Lybster Church, we laid Margaret to rest in the graveyard at Latheron, below the historic Gunn Clan Memorial.

It is so pretty there, with its glorious views down the coast beyond Dunbeath. A gentle rain softened the green land and the picturesque sea cliffs. The mighty North Sea, all misty and grey and sombre, reflected the mood of us all, for Margaret was well loved in the Kirk and in the village.

I still have an occasional nutmilk chocolate and I still think of her.

Chapter 29

Altimarlach: The Field of Gory

One afternoon Janet and I went out to see George and Kathy.

George had been the first person I'd visited in Wick hospital, and it was good to see him now, fully restored to health. He and Kathy were regular members of the Lybster congregation and we'd come to know them quite well, and had visited their home before.

George was the cleverest engineer I have ever met. Nothing seemed beyond his capable hands, and there were many evidences of his skill around the property, including a magnificent, working waterwheel. His specialty was the making of perfectly proportioned scale model, radio-controlled ships and boats which he started from scratch, up to two metres in length. They were all models of former vessels. He even made the tiny fittings, such as portholes and pulleys, all in perfect proportion.

I, on the other hand, am the exact opposite in matters practical. I sometimes tell people that I am not able to do this or that because I was born with an unfortunate deformity – eleven thumbs.

That day, as we sat chatting with our teas and scones in their pleasant sunroom, George suddenly asked, "Have you heard of Altimarlach?"

It was George who'd first told us about the Whalego steps. He had a keen interest in the history of Caithness and was happy to share his knowledge.

We shook our heads. "Never heard of it, George," I told him; "is it a type of Scottish shortbread biscuit, or something?"

He smiled. "No – it's a place with a fascinating but very sad history."

We waited as George settled himself into his chair.

"Altimarlach," continued our host, "is the site of the last clan battle in Scotland – and it's no' sae very far from here. It's well worth a visit."

I was interested. I leaned forward in my chair. "It sounds fascinating. What does that strange name, Altimarlach, mean, George?"

"It's Gaelic in origin of course, as is the name of this property, as you know. The name Altimarlach goes back a long way in history, and in the Gaelic it's called Allt Nam Méirleach, or in English, "The Burn of the Robbers." As you know, a burn is a Scottish word for a stream, or brook. In time the Gaelic name was anglicised to Altimarlach."

"And that's where the last clan battle in Scotland was fought?"

"Aye – it was, on 13 July, 1680. Of course, it was all to do with money, property - that sort of thing.

The story goes that George Sinclair, the 6th earl of Caithness, owed Sir John Campbell a great deal of money, which he couldn't repay, and in the end, Campbell foreclosed and Sinclair was forced to surrender his title, his lands and property to the Campbells. Suddenly the Sinclairs were title-less, homeless and penniless! Sir John Campbell was now Earl of Caithness.

When George Sinclair died a few months later, his successor, whose name was also George Sinclair, disputed the claim of the Campbells and seized back the old Sinclair lands.

Of course, the Campbells were not going to take that lying doon!

Two years later, Campbell assembled a force of eight hundred men and marched to Caithness to evict the Sinclairs from what he saw as his rightful property.

The Sinclairs were waiting for them, but had only about five hundred men as opposed to eight hundred Campbells.

To make matters worse, the night before the battle commenced, the Sinclairs hit the bottle – or so the story goes.

The next day, well-fuelled with good Highland whisky and in no condition to fight, they attacked the Campbells at Altimarlach, with disastrous results. It was said at the time that for two days, the river Wick, which flows below the hill at Altimarlach, ran red wi' the blood o' the Sinclairs."

"What a story!" I exclaimed, "And how tragic. What happened after that?"

"The Campbells took possession and Sir John Campbell claimed the title of Earl of Caithness once more."

"And that was that? End of story?"

"Not at all! The Sinclairs," continued George, "were seething at the defeat, and George Sinclair, knowing that he couldn't defeat the Campbells in battle, took the fight to the Scottish High Court.

It was a time when clan battles were becoming unpopular, and frowned upon by the law, and the court saw fit to support the Sinclair claim. Within a couple of years, the property was handed back to the Sinclairs legally and George Sinclair reclaimed his title as Earl of Caithness.

O' course, Sir John Campbell was outraged, but he was appeased when he was made Earl of Breadalbane."

"I wonder if the Sinclairs ever repaid the debt of money they owed the Campbells?"

George smiled and shook his head. "I'm afraid that's a question I cannae answer, Lachlan."

"Oh well," I said, "I suppose in a way it all ended happily ever after – if one can forget the hundreds of grieving families who lost their husbands, fathers and sons in the battle. By the way, is there anything up there to see now?"

"There certainly is!" declared George. "Many years ago, a large cross was built on the site of the battle. That's why it would be a very interesting place for you to visit."

"How would we get there?"

"Simple! Go into Wick, to the park by Somerville's supermarket down by the river. At the edge of the park there is a big roadside map of the district. It will tell you how to get there."

We were determined to visit Altimarlach, and the following Saturday provided the opportunity, for there was nothing in the diary.

Several people we spoke to told us it wasn't a long walk, although no one we knew seemed to have been there.

On Saturday morning we were in Wick, where, as George said it would be, we found a large tourist map of the area, and details of how to get to Altimarlach.

"It certainly looks simple enough," Janet observed as we studied the billboard-sized map. "We start right here, where we're standing, and follow that path that goes along this side of the river, and finally we should get there. According to the map, Altimarlach is not far from the river, but upstream."

Cheerfully we set off, following the concrete walking path.

We had been walking for some time when we saw a lady approaching, with a dog on a lead.

"Excuse me," I asked, "would you know how far it is to Altimarlach?"

She shook her head. "I'm sorry – I can't help you, but from what I am told, it no' very far from here."

I thanked her and we walked on. I was surprised we'd had to walk so far, with no sign that we were anywhere near our destination.

A man approached on the path and I stopped to ask him if we had far to go. "No, not at all!" he told us: "just keep following the path you're on and you'll be there in no time."

Heartened at this information, we walked on. We'd already been walking for an hour, along a path that was gradually steepening.

Suddenly, the walking path stopped. Before us was a rather narrow, muddy track. On the right side was a fence, while the other side fell away rather steeply to where we could see the river Wick far below, looking like a sliver of silver. It was obvious why it was called a burn, for so far up there it was no more than creek-sized.

We stopped, nonplussed.

"We can't have far to go!" I exclaimed. "The map definitely showed that Altimarlach is not far from the river. We'll have to go on now – we can't stop now that we've come this far."

We trudged on in single file, which was all the narrow track would allow. It was sloppy from recent rain, and the footprints in it told us that nothing but sheep had passed that way recently.

Some considerable time later, the hill flattened out and we could see a farm house to our right. "We must be nearly there now!" Janet sounded exhausted.

"There it is!" I called excitedly: "I can see the cross, off to the left, in the distance."

Janet looked. "Thank heavens! I didn't think we were ever going to get there. We must have walked miles, and most of it uphill at that."

We set off, our spirits renewed, walking up another hill. When we reached the grassy top, we saw another hill in front of us.

"That's funny," I said; "I can see the cross, but it doesn't seem to be any closer."

We walked down the hill and were dismayed to see a bog at the bottom. A search soon revealed there was no place narrow enough to jump across. We'd have to wade through it.

Janet sat down in the grass. "I can't go on any further. I'm not going to wade through that, and there may be more. I'll stay here. You have the camera. Bring me back a photo."

I looked at her, concerned. "Are you sure? Are you OK?"

"I'm fine. I just can't walk any more. Off you go."

I could see Janet did not intend to go further, so set off. I walked through the bog and laboriously made my way up the next hill. There was yet another hill in front of me – and the cross did not appear any closer at all. Resignedly, and with a stubbornness born of increasing irritability, I walked on. There was a stone fence across the land, which I climbed over. It occurred to me it was highly unlikely that whoever made up the map on the billboard back at Wick had ever made the trip in person and had no real idea of how to get to Altimarlach.

At the bottom of the hill I found another bog, which I plunged through. I looked down at my trousers, which were covered in dark mud. Janet, I said to myself, had made the right decision!

At the top of the next hill the cross was now plainly visible, beyond a curtain of low gorse. With renewed energy I walked on, and at last I was within yards of my goal, just the other side of the gorse

I arrived at the gorse, and stopped in disbelief. The gorse hid a fence, and on the other side of the fence was a narrow, sheer, impassable gorge, dropping out of sight. There was no way I was going to be able to stand beside that cross! This was it. I knew that at least I could take a telephoto picture of the cross, and that's what I did.

It was what is known as a Celtic Cross, of weathered grey stone.

I could see that there must be another way to it, for the ground was flat on the other side, but having been there, it was enough. If ever we go back to Caithness, I thought, we'll try to get to Altimarlach by another way.

I made my way back to Janet over the hills and the stone fence and through the bogs, and sat down wearily beside her. She'd befriended three horses that had come to see who the stranger was.

She took in my muddy appearance. "Lachlan – you're a mess!"

I certainly was, and could feel my trousers clinging coldly and muddily to me. The wind was strong, and I was cold.

She was impressed with the photo I took of the cross.

"I could see you as you walked away, getting smaller and smaller until you disappeared from sight. I'm glad I decided not to go. I can't get over that man, telling us we didn't have much farther to go."

"Oh well, if he'd told us we'd a long way to go, maybe we'd have turned back. At least, we made it. I recall reading a book, many years ago, about Australia and Australians. It was written about the turn of the twentieth century and there are two things in particular I remember from that book. First, the writer said that Australians in general didn't like walking. He said they'd walk a mile to catch a horse to ride a mile."

"And the second?"

He wrote that if someone was walking between towns and didn't know how far it was to the next, and asked a local, he, not wanting to discourage the walker, would say it was four miles, when he really thought it was eight miles, while the actual distance was sixteen miles. Maybe the man we spoke to thought like that."

Janet looked dubious. "Perhaps. Personally, I don't think he had a clue just how far it was."

"It doesn't matter now anyway," I said. "It's a long way back. Let's go."

It was easier on the way back, for it was mainly downhill, and as well we knew approximately how long it would take us.

The burn further up in the hills that we had seen near Altimarlach, which was in fact the young river Wick, becomes a wide and beautiful river by the time it arrives at the town, flowing under the picturesque road bridge, into the harbour and out into the sea.

When we got back to the car Janet looked at me. "There's no way you can get into the car like that Lach. We'd never get the mud off the seat. As well, we've not long had the car to that garage, where we cleaned it inside and out."

"Are you suggesting I should drive home naked?"

She giggled. "No – I think there's a table cloth in the boot that we take on picnics, and a towel. We'll cover the seat with those."

With the driver's seat well covered, we set off. As we drove, thoughts of the next day's sermon were on my mind. I was not happy with it. Things needed to be done to it…

I looked at the fuel gauge. It was down to a third. Just ahead, I could see a roadside garage, so pulled in beside the diesel bowser. As I got out I could see the attendant watching me through his window in the building. "He's probably looking at the muddy apparition, wondering what it is," I thought.

The bowser had a hose at either end and a gauge either side in the manner of all fuel bowsers, and as I started to fill, someone pulled up on the other side and started using the other hose.

Thoughts of the service were on my mind... changes to be made...

The hose clicked to a stop to indicate a full tank so I hung it up.

There was a sudden shout from the garage attendant, who was walking out. "Hey - you hung up your hose at the wrong end of the bowser!" he called.

I looked at him stupidly. "What?"

"Your fuel hose. You hung it up on the end that other person's using!"

The other driver had just finished and was holding his fuel hose, looking at us.

Suddenly I realised what I'd done. "Oh – sorry!" and lifted the hose back off to put it my end, vaguely aware as I did so of the attendant's urgent "Stop – don't do that!" followed by "Ah, hell!"

Again I found myself holding the fuel hose while staring stupidly at the attendant. "What?"

The attendant's complexion had turned red. "When you lifted the hose off, the meter rolled back to zero for the next customer. Now I don't know how much this other gentleman used! Did you happen to notice the amount on the meter?"

I thought for a moment. "I think it was £31.00."

The other driver nodded. "Yes, it was about that, Don. Make it £32,00, to be on the safe side."

What a decent, honest man, I thought; and they know each other, so he's not likely to be trying to rip off the attendant.

Their eyes were on me, no doubt taking in the mud-caked clothing and the hair dishevelled by the high cold winds of Altimarlach.

I sheepishly paid for my fuel, thanked the other driver and left.

In the rear vision mirror I could see the other driver and Don the attendant standing together, staring after me. Don was shaking his head.

"I don't think that little incident did anything for Scotto-Australian relations," I remarked to Janet.

She had been an interested observer of all that had taken place.

We drove on for a while, heading for Lybster, the warm manse, a welcome shower and a change of clothes.

My thoughts were still on various adjustments I needed to make to the following day's service.

Janet's voice broke into my thoughts. "Lachlan," she said kindly, "I fear there are times when that little world you seem to live in from time to time, actually takes over."

Chapter 30

Dunrobin

It was an early morning in May as we sat in the kitchen, having breakfast. The radio was tuned into the Gaelic station, and a sweet Gaelic song was filling the air around us. I was vaguely aware that at the same time, Janet was reading aloud from a pamphlet. Sometimes, when I am trying to listen to music that I'm really enjoying, Janet will be absorbed in something completely different, telling me all about it, completely oblivious of the music, and that day was one of those occasions. Over the years I have learned to have my antennae finely tuned, and to make appropriate sounds while not giving Janet's words the attention they deserved. Good old standbys that have stood the test of time are "Really?" or "How sad!" Or "How funny" or "Dear me..." When I misjudge occasionally and utter "How sad!" when I should have replied, "That's wonderful news! Have they chosen a name? Are they both well?" The accusation is usually "You haven't heard a word I've said!" Of course it's true, or mostly true, so I am forced to think back feverishly for clues as to what she may have been telling me.

On that morning, as Janet read from the pamphlet, I just happened to catch the words "Dunrobin Castle" so quickly decided it would be in my best interests to tune in. "Listen to this," Janet was saying. "It says Dunrobin Castle has been called home to the Earls and Dukes of Sutherland since the 13th century. The Earldom of Sutherland was created in 1235 and a castle appears to have stood on this site since then, possibly on the site of an early medieval fort. The name Dun Robin means Robin's Hill or Fort in Gaelic and may have come from Robert, the 6th Earl of Sutherland who died in 1427 . . .

My wife raised her head to look at me, and I was glad that I gave the impression of having been listening intently all along.

"Lach," Janet said, "when Merran brought us in some eggs the other day, she gave me this pamphlet. Dunrobin Castle is only a short drive down to Golspie – less than an hour, I'm told. I think we should go. After all," she reminded me, "it's not as if we will be in Scotland for the rest of our lives, so we should see as many of the local places of interest we can. Merran told me we should make a point of seeing the castle. She told me it's full of memorabilia dating back centuries."

It was a persuasive argument. I myself had been told we should make a point of visiting Dunrobin Castle. Like so many other attractions, it closes during the winter months, but is open to tourists in spring and summer.

What had finally convinced me were the tales I'd heard of the falconing demonstrations held at the castle.

A few days later we made our way south into the county of Sutherland. As usual, the beauty of the hills utterly captivated us, and the warm day held a promise of things to come. "Aye," someone had replied when I'd mentioned the warming weather, "but the Maygobs can sometimes spring a surprise – you mark my words!"

"The Maygobs," he added, obviously noting my blank look, "is a bitingly cold wind, often bringing snow, that arrives in May - just when we think winter is over for another year – it's a Caithness word."

There was no indication of approaching Maygobs that fine spring morning. "I can't get over the richness of the gorse on the hills," Janet exclaimed as we travelled south.

"Someone told me that up in our part of Scotland, it's called whins, not gorse," I told her.

In well under an hour we turned off at the castle gates and made our way in. Quite a few other cars were already parked, so we knew the Sutherlands were enjoying a host of visitors. As we gazed at the magnificence of the great castle, the expense of keeping such a residence crossed my mind. I guessed that that was the reason why the castle was open to paying visitors, but we were glad the Sutherlands were prepared to open their beautiful castle to all, for what was not a great sum. We paid our £7.00 each and made our way through gardens of exquisite beauty to where the falconer was demonstrating before a large, seated crowd. We glanced back at the castle. The front facing the road had been imposing. The rear, facing the east, was spectacularly magnificent. Numerous, elegant round towers rose above countless windows in a display of mediaeval splendour. Never had we colonials seen the like. The falconer was demonstrating the ability of a magnificent European eagle owl named Cedar. He was amazing. His beauty, his strength, his intelligence, his ability to fly in complete silence left us all open-mouthed. The falconer loved the bird and it showed. Cedar also showed his affection for that remarkable man. I managed to have a chat to the falconer and some other staff members, and was told there is a possibility that eagle owls may be breeding in various parts of Scotland, including Sutherland. They said the birds are not native to Britain but may be migrating from Europe.

During and after the demonstration, Cedar sat sociably on a bench among the delighted onlookers, but we were warned not to touch him. One look at that formidable beak would have convinced anyone. Cedar, we were told, is very placid, but no one disobeyed the warning! I was fascinated as I looked closely at that remarkable creature, with his yellow eyes and the 'horns' above his head. As I looked, I could see how owls over the centuries have earned a reputation as wise creatures. Cedar looked wise.

Afterwards, we went up to the castle itself and were free to walk through the twenty rooms and along the wide corridors open to tourists. The corridor walls were lined with beautiful paintings of various members of the clan, dating back many centuries.

Each room was different, each full of rare and lovely paintings, wall hangings, antique furniture, each room breathing a glorious past.

We spoke to one of the attendants who told us that there were quarters in the castle for family members, but most have private residences somewhere on the estate of 20,000 acres.

Finally we left, and made our way down to the town where we enjoyed a sandwich at a picnic table by the North Sea. In the distance we could see the flashing light from the lighthouse on Tarbat Ness, away to the south east. A chilly wind had sprung up out of the North Sea by this time, so we did not linger over lunch.

Towering above Golspie, on top of Ben Bragghie is the massive 130ft high memorial of the 1st Earl of Sutherland. The statue of the man dominates the town and district.

We were told that the Earl himself was despised by the people of his day, for, we were told, he was responsible for the Highland Clearances in that area back in the 1830's, when great numbers of crofter tenants were removed from their crofts to make way for sheep, which it was believed would prove more profitable than rent from the crofts.

On the way home, not far from the bounds of our parish, Janet suddenly called "Stop!" She'd seen a sign that I'd missed. We turned back a short distance, where we saw a sign that read "Badbea."

"I remember reading about that place," Janet told me, so we parked the car to read the writing under the sign. We learned that not far away, on the edge of a cliff overlooking the sea, stood the remnants of the abandoned and sad village of Badbea.

It was there that former crofter tenants, removed from their land, were forced to eke out a pitiful existence. "It's not far," said Janet; "Let's have a look." We walked along a narrow, muddy track over peaty, desolate moorland, right to the edge of the great cliffs overlooking the sea, where the village once stood. Now, almost nothing remains, apart from a stone memorial. It is a tragic place, and a sad aura hangs over it. The winds there can blow with such ferocity that the children had to be tethered, to prevent them from being blown over the cliff into the sea; a fate met by many animals.

It gave us something to think about as we continued our journey home; comparing the wealth and power of many of the Scottish lairds of that time and the pitiful plight of the residents of Badbea.

I had been quite intrigued by Cedar the eagle owl and when I thought about it that night it occurred to me that owls have always held a fascination for me. They are very difficult to see, for they are mainly nocturnal creatures.

I had no idea of an encounter that was to occur later that week.

Chapter 31

The owl

I could hardly believe it when, a couple of evenings after our visit to Dunrobin Castle, I walked out into the manse garden and saw an owl, silhouetted in the light of a full moon that rode low behind him, watching me from the branch of a low tree. I stopped, lost in the breathtaking beauty of the scene before me, aware that at any moment it could disappear in a cloud across the moon, or on the wings of the owl.

Memory of my last owl encounter came flooding back. Early one morning while walking along the shore of Lake Macquarie, not far from our home, I saw some frantic movement on the ground, and when I went to investigate, found a large owl, hopelessly entangled in fishing line. I could see it was fast becoming exhausted. One look at the powerful beak was enough to make me take off my jacket, which I wrapped around the owl, leaving enough of him visible to start removing the fishing line.

The owl was suspicious of my motives and slashed viciously at the jacket with his beak, but at last he was free. I threw him into the air, where he flew sluggishly into a tree, and remained there for the rest of the day, doubtless waiting for nightfall.

The owl at the Lybster manse showed no particular inclination to fly away, so I remained where I was, wishing the scene would remain forever. I wasn't sure what to do, so decided to engage him in conversation: "I once saved one of your kind," I told him, "a long, long way from here. I was walking by the lake where we live, early one morning, when I saw an owl, badly tangled in fishing line. I managed to free him and watch him fly away."

The owl received the information with seeming indifference; in fact I gained the impression that he didn't give a hoot what I'd done to aid a fellow owl several years ago and 20,000 kilometres away.

"Don't you care that I saved one of your kind?" I persisted; "Don't you think you should give thanks for that?"

The owl appeared to ponder my question before replying with one of his own: To who? he asked me; To who?

"To God, Who created you, and all around you!" I told him, motioning with my arm.

The owl, probably disturbed by the movement, or perhaps bored by my company, suddenly stretched his wings and departed, was silhouetted briefly in the light of the great moon, then disappeared, lost among the stars in the darkling sky.

Later in the evening, as I reflected on the owl's visit to our garden, a little poem popped into my head, the way they sometimes do after some particular incident, so I jotted it down:

The Owl

One eve at Lybster manse
I saw it – just by chance:
A lone owl in a garden tree.
His round, all-knowing eyes,
Inscrutable and wise
Were gazing quite intently down on me.
No single word I heard
From the still and silent bird
In the tree just by the garden wall,
So I told a little joke,
Yet not a word he spoke –
No hoot or who or other owly call.
Then overjoyed was I
To catch a brief reply
As he took off in the gath'ring gloom.
But that wise and clever bird
Had grammatically erred:
His 'to who' should have been 'to whom.'

The following morning Janet walked into the study as I did a little polishing on the poem. "Are you starting your sermon?" she asked.

"No," I replied, "I'm making a change or two, to a little poem I jotted down last night. Have a look at this."

My wife took it and read it through. She is a very good judge of anything I write and I've always valued her thoughts.

"Hmmm, it's very nice," she told me, "but that line 'grammatically erred' isn't easy to read. The metre seems wrong."

I held out my hand for the paper. "Gimme a look."

I read the lines in question. "I see what you mean. The trouble is, you are pronouncing 'grammatically' as 'grammaticly.' Pronounce it as it is written: 'grammati-cally' Then it scans."

Janet looked doubtful. "It seems a bit complicated to me. I wonder if Wordsworth and Tennyson and all the rest had the same problem?"

I had to smile. "Thank you for mentioning me in the same breath as those great heroes of English literature, my dear. This poem however is only a bit of fun, and not worthy of any mention, honourable or otherwise."

All the same, I wished that I could communicate, as they did, a thought to touch the soul, as the sight of the owl did for me that night, when I could see and marvel at a tiny fraction of the miracle that is God's creation.

Chapter 32

Parish doings

Spring turned to summer, and all nature continued to rejoice in the beauty of the earth, the beauty of the sky.

I took the opportunity to continue my visiting regime, for the parish had been without a minister for so long that many had forgotten what it was like simply to have a minister drop in on a casual basis, neither bearing bad news nor calling at a sick bed. Everyone spoke highly of the work that John the deacon had performed. Even when stretched to the limit, he'd made time to sit and talk wherever possible.

There wasn't a day went past when I didn't have some story, funny or sad, to tell Janet.

One day my visiting took me to the croft home of Ewing and Audrey Anderson, both well on the other side of seventy.

They were walking over to where I could see some hens scratching in a fowl yard when I arrived, and I noted with some surprise that they were holding hands.

They changed direction and came to greet me at the gate, still holding hands.

When I introduced myself, Mrs Anderson held out her hand. "We heard we might get a visit from you, Mr Ness. Please, come in - it's almost afternoon tea time now." She was small, fair and roundish, with a bright smile and merry eyes.

Her husband was tall and thickset, and looked to be quite a serious man, but I could see the humour in his dark eyes when he smiled.

We sat in their cosy parlour and chatted over our tea, from matters of faith to family concerns. They had many questions about Australia, for they'd rarely been outside the county of Caithness.

They sat together on a two-seater lounge, and every now and then I saw Mr Anderson's hand sneak over and take his wife's hand.

"I think you told me you've been married fifty years next year," I commented, "and after all that time, you still like to hold hands. I think that's rather lovely."

Ewing Anderson threw me a rather sheepish smile. "Aye, well, there's a story behind here. Audrey and I grew up together, y'ken, and I always fancied her – and I wasn't the only one, I can tell you! She was a very pretty gurrl, and a lot o' the young fellas in the district around here felt about her as I did – particularly my best friend, Norm McFoxley. In fact he was my main rival.

One evening, when we were teenagers, there was a concert in Wick. Audrey's parents wanted to go so invited Norm and me to go with them and Audrey. Of course we accepted wi' alacrity!

It was a great concert too – not that I remember much about it now. I spent a lot of it just looking at Audrey and thinking how pretty she was.

Came time to come home. We three young ones were in the back seat of the old Austin with a rug over our laps, for it was awfu' cold, and there were few cars with heaters in those days. Audrey was in the middle, between us two boys.

Our hands were under the rug for warmth, and all I wanted to do was hold hers, to let her know how I felt about her, so I sneaked my hand along under the rug, looking for hers."

I glanced at Audrey. She was trying to repress a giggle.

"Suddenly, I felt it! I closed my hand over it and was surprised to find my hand given a little squeeze. 'Hullo! I thought to myself, "I think she really fancies me!'

I squeezed back. I can't tell you how I felt when there was another, answering squeeze – I felt as if all my Christmases and birthdays had been rolled into one, and I was in dreamland. I could have stayed in the car forever. There we sat, all the way back home, with me in raptures. As we got near the village, Audrey withdrew her hands from under the rug and placed them on top.

The trouble was – I was still holding a hand! I stared, aghast, at Norm. He was staring, aghast, at me!

It dawned on us at the same time – Norm and I had been holding each other's hand - and all the way from Wick!

Talk aboot disgusted! Och, well, in the end, Audrey married me, and Norm found a lovely girl called Joy, and they've been happily married these many years too.

From then on, I told myself, I'm going to make sure it's Audrey's hand I hold, whenever I can!"

I was still chortling on the way home, and could hardly wait to tell Janet.

Later, when I reflected on Ewing's story, it occurred to me that Ewing and Audrey had found true married happiness by living their life together as God intended it to be, for life lived in the spirit of love always protects, always trusts, always hopes, always perseveres. 1 Cor 13:7 (NIV).

I sat in front of my laptop computer in the study one evening, working away busily on the "Minister's Message," getting it ready for the following day, when all the material for the church order of service had to be in, ready for printing.

How wonderful, I thought as I typed, are these computers! What a change from the old, primitive clunker typewriters of my day!

I paused to read through what I'd typed. Hmmm… that paragraph I've just typed would be better-suited a couple of paragraphs up, rather than here. No worries, no need to re-type! It's so easy these days… highlight the paragraph, control-x to delete, put the cursor where the deleted paragraph is to go and click the mouse. Hit control-v and voila! Suddenly the deleted paragraph reappears exactly where I want it. Amazing!

Something made me feel a little uncomfortable when I was carrying out my own instructions, and suddenly I realised what it was… the letter X I'd just used.

My thoughts ranged back many years, to a parish a long time ago, in Australia.

It had been a marvellous parish, but as is the case with just about any parish, there is usually someone who appears to have been sent to make life a little more challenging.

My challenge was in the form of Miss Gertrude Coutts; a thin, hard-nosed, busybody of a woman known as Gertie among most, but among those more kindly disposed as Trudy. To her credit, Miss Coutts served on just about every committee in the town and was always concerned for the less fortunate, some of whom would have preferred to remain less fortunate rather than have to front those piercing blue eyes and that sharp tongue. She'd been a school teacher, known to be well-read and very clever, as well as a little mad. Many of the locals who'd had Miss Coutts as a teacher had their own tales to tell.

She was also a regular attender at church, but meetings were always more difficult when she was on a committee for this or that, for she challenged practically every decision the committee made, and seemed to enjoy being the sole dissenting voice. Again, to her credit, if anyone was needed for a task in the church, Miss Coutts was always the first to volunteer.

I enjoyed a cordial if somewhat wary relationship with Miss Coutts, for there were various committees on which we both served, and she spoke her mind regardless. It was well-known that she disliked men and was always suspicious of their motives. The weakness of the flesh rated high on Miss Coutts's long list of unforgiveable sins. A kindly word could be misconstrued as an unwelcome advance.

One day there was to be a meeting of the Church Ladies' Guild at the home of Norma, the Guild's president. I'd been asked to chair it, for it was an annual meeting.

I was the first there. The front door was open, waiting for the meeting's members to arrive, so I wandered in, where Norma was making some sandwiches for morning tea. We'd no sooner greeted each other when the family cat, Meg, knowing I love cats, brushed herself, purring, against my leg. I looked down.

"Oh, you are so beautiful!" I said, bending to give her a pat.

I'd no sooner straightened when I heard a step behind me and turning, observed Miss Coutts, who had just walked in. She'd obviously heard what I'd just said.

Her sharp old eyes, glinting behind her spectacles, flitted from Norma back to me.

Her voice was brittle with suspicion: "I hope I'm not interrupting something here."

"Of course not!" I replied hotly; "I was talking to Meg, the cat." I looked to where Meg had been. Miss Coutts's eyes followed mine. Of course there was no cat. Meg, having paid her respects, had wandered out of the room. I felt my colour deepen by several degrees.

Norma, who was always jolly and good natured, began to laugh at the incongruity of it all. I think Miss Coutts saw that as an indication of guilt.

From then on, Miss Coutts's eye was upon me. I was a marked man.

Those were pre-computer days and I had an old clunker of a Remington typewriter that required a heavy hand on the keys to make any impression at all on the paper. It had been good in its day, but that day was long past.

In those days, if one made a mistake while typing, one had to start again, or use a liquid called 'white-out' to blot out the error and type over it, or in the absence of 'white-out' use the letter X to indicate an error, and start the word again. All my typing work was covered in Xs because my lack of dexterity made me an eleven-thumbed typist. I was always running out of white-out.

One day I typed up a list of duties for an up and coming church fete. On the bottom, I'd typed in capitals:

THESE ARRANGMENTS ARE IN THE HANDS OF MISS GERTRUDE COUTTS.

I looked at my work. It was not good. I'd run out of white-out and there were Xs everywhere. Still, I didn't have time to start again.

Laboriously, I duplicated the notice on the primitive church duplicator: one copy for each member of the congregation, to be handed out at church the following Sunday morning.

On Sunday afternoon, directly after lunch, I had a phone call. It was Miss Coutts. She did not sound happy, and she had a surprising query.

"Mr Ness, have you heard of Sigmund Freud, the father of psycho-analysis?"

"Well, yes" I replied, wondering where this query was leading; "In fact we studied some of his work in pastoral psychology, when I was a student for the ministry."

"In that case you will be familiar with what is known as the 'Freudian slip'?"

"That's like a so-called 'slip of the tongue,' isn't it, Miss Coutts? Freud wrote that whatever was said was really a repressed wish coming out and so wasn't a 'slip' at all. He seemed to apply it a lot to sexual innuendo."

"Congratulations, Mr Ness," replied Miss Coutts silkily; "I'm pleased to see you remember something of what you learned."

I chose to ignore the veiled insult. "Are you writing a paper on Freud, or something, Miss Coutts? Can I help you in some way?"

"Yes – you can help. You can help me by not looking upon me as a possible conquest, Mr Ness. Good afternoon!"

Before I could utter a word, she'd hung up.

I stared, dumbfounded, at the dead phone in my hand.

I went find Janet, to tell her of the astonishing conversation with Miss Coutts, when I heard the front door bang and Janet came in. She'd been laughing.

"Lach, I've just been talking to Mrs McKenzie across the road. She pointed out something in that paper you handed out after church. She says the whole congregation is in hysterics – everyone, that is, except Miss Coutts. Everyone who hasn't seen it wants a copy. Get yours and I'll show you what I mean."

She showed me, and I groaned. It was on the bottom line that I'd typed in capitals. At first I'd failed to put a space between 'these' and 'arrangements' ('thesearrangements') and had covered the 'a' with an X before starting again – and it stood out in glaring detail:

"THESE ARRANGEMENTS ARE IN THE HANDS OF MISS COUTTS" had become, via my clumsy hand:

"THESE̶X̶ ARRANGEMENTS ARE IN THE HANDS OF MISS COUTTS."

I never did quite manage to live it down. Members of the congregation would refer to it jocularly from time to time, for it had become a standing joke, while Miss Coutts regarded me with even deeper suspicion.

It was like that until I had a call to another parish a couple of years later.

Oh well, I thought, it's a long time gone in the distant past, not to mention a long way away in distant Australia…

Highlight the text, hit control-x, put the cursor where I want the deleted text to appear. Click, and hit Control-v and the text magically appears in its new location. Nothing could be easier.

It's too bad people aren't always so easy to deal with…

In Australia, basking in the warmth of the South Pacific, the changing seasons seem to arrive a little diffidently, even reluctantly, but up here in the far North of Scotland, the change from snow and winter gales to green fields seems to happen with magical suddenness.

One June day, as I drove along the winding roads and looked out to hills dotted white with sheep and young lambs, it occurred to me that the warmer days are not here for very long at latitude 59 degrees north. Nature has to work at desperate speed to get everything accomplished before the return of wintry days.

There was no one at home at many of the crofts I visited, but I always left a card and a cheery note to let the folk know I'd been. Often, both husband and wife were out "lambing," helping the woolly mothers deliver their babies.

At one remote croft, two young children were playing in the front garden.

"Hullo!" I called from the fence, "Is either your mum or your dad home?"

They stopped their game to regard me shyly before shaking their heads.

"Are they very far away?"

"Och, no," the older boy replied, "They're doon the fields. The coos are bullin'."

I smiled as I drove away. The cows were with the bulls and everywhere nature was reproducing and recreating.

All was just as it should be, although I doubt if Miss Coutts would have approved.

Chapter 33

Summer's golden days

One day, summer arrived in Britain and was followed by a flurry of activity, both in nature and among the human race.

Festivals sprang up everywhere, seemingly like mushrooms, from Land's End to John o' Groats. Little tea houses and cafes that had been closed during the winter months once again opened their doors; among them the charming "Waterlines" down at Lybster harbour. It was a small museum of the great herring days, with a pleasant little café attached. Janet and I had been down to visit both the excellent museum and enjoy the café. We had sat on a seat outside with our tea and home-made cake, looking out to the little harbour and its picturesque fishing boats, while beyond the grey stone harbour-wall rolled the solemn waters of the North Sea.

One day a convoy of gaily decorated 1960's Mini Minors pulled up in Lybster's main street. The drivers and passengers were all decked out as flower power people, and the Minis themselves were painted with flowers and symbols of the fabulous 1960s. They were off to the annual Wick Festival, which started that day.

With summer, the once-quiet roads were full of traffic: motor-bikers doing the annual Land's End to John o' Groats pilgrimage, sharing the road with motor homes, caravans, push-bikes and walkers, all doing the same thing. One had to be alert on the roads to avoid them.

As well, crazed city dwellers from down south arrived like migrating geese, apparently unaware that our normally quiet rural county, with

its narrow, winding roads and little country lanes, must be shared
with tractors and other farm implements, sheep, cows, straying chooks,
horses, as well as the odd teuchter out rounding them up.

Mother Nature too seemed to have sprung to life, bright-eyed and
bushy-tailed. The grass and leaves, with almost 24 hours of daylight to
play with, were bursting with greens so deep and rich as to challenge
one's imagination, especially for us colonials from country NSW, for
whom green usually means olive green.

Birds and small animals were everywhere. In summer, deer roam the
woods with rabbits, porcupines and other small creatures. Sometimes
they venture onto the roads, frequently with fatal consequences. Once, a
Scottish wildcat ran across the road in front of me. They are considerably
larger than domestic cats and have quite a feral look about them. I was
amazed to see it, for they are rarely seen. The sky was full of the sweet
carolling of birds as nature did her utmost to make the most of the short
northern summer.

Lybster, not to be outdone, had its own Gala Week. It was all the
fun of the fair: the floats, the crowds (big, for Lybster), the colourful
outfits, the pipes, the Scottish dancing, the crowning of the Lybster
Gala Queen.

A month before the Gala Week was due to start, Lyn, one of the
organisers, had approached me and asked if Janet and I would be
prepared to judge the floats. I had been both moved and horrified when
asked; moved by the fact that the locals had not only so graciously and
warmly welcomed Janet and me, but were also prepared to bestow upon
us the honour of judging the floats. My horror simply came from the
thought of carrying out the difficult task of choosing what we, and
perhaps not others, considered the best float.

On the big day, when Janet and I wandered to the village hall to
check on when we should start judging the floats we were told that
we would also be judging the children's Fancy Dress! I was even more
horrified. Judging the floats was going to be bad enough – but the
children…! We knew every child would have worked for hours on the
task of creating a costume, from pirate to fairy, and so it turned out
to be.

Just before the children were to be paraded, I rushed up to Lyn, the
organiser: "Lyn – do you think it would be possible to institute a new
category – one where none of the children would be disappointed?"

The organiser looked surprised. "Possibly. What do have in mind?"
"Highly Commended."

Lyn's eyes lit up. "Great idea! I'll organise some little gifts" and she hurried off.

Amid a lot of noise and cheering, the gaily decorated children were paraded before the spectators, and after a lot of thought, we chose what we thought was the best fancy dress. All the others received a 'highly commended' prize. It was a great success.

From there we went off to judge the floats, with Karen, one of the locals, to help us. The numerous floats were all magnificent, and much humour was displayed by some of the creators. Again, after a great deal of thought, we made a choice – but it was hard!

Finally we repaired to the brightly decorated village hall. It was a true country scene: kids and parents everywhere, including the occasional dog with its human family. There was a tea/coffee and cake stall: 50p a touch, so I went off to buy one each for us.

The lady at the serving table looked at me. "Och, no, no!" she said. "You're on the TOP table – you'll be getting served the noo." (the noo = now).

I looked at the top table and again was smitten with horror. The Gala Queen and all her resplendent entourage were there! I have always avoided, where possible, being part of the limelight. At the same time however, I was reminded that Janet and I were being accorded a singular honour. It would be churlish and indeed rude, not to accept the honour with the same graciousness with which it was bestowed. There was nothing for it.

We had not long seated ourselves when Lyn returned and beckoned us. "Here's your next job," she informed us; "You're to hand the prizes to the Gala Queen who will hand them to the winners." We stood up on the stage as the winners' names were called. I did one lot and Janet the next. Finally, it was over.

Then Lyn stood. "On behalf of the Gala committee I'd like to thank Mr and Mrs Ness, our judges..." (clapping) "and accept these tokens of our thanks."

We were handed a box of chocs, a bouquet of flowers and a bottle of wine.

Looking back, it was all such a lot of fun, and we were thrilled to discover how warmly and quickly we had been accepted by the community as part of it.

There were other indications too, and I was reminded of it the following day when I opened the refrigerator door and saw the large quantity of eggs, given to me during my visits to the farms and homes around the district. The eggs were really delicious, for they were the product of real free-range chooks that scratch contentedly around farm or back yard and probably die eventually of old age.

Chapter 34

Ullapool and beyond

Summer continued to advance, and as the wintry days began to lose their cold grip on the country, we noticed an increasing number of visitors in the pews on Sundays, both at Dunbeath and Lybster; mostly from other parts of the realm but also from overseas. It was always a delight to greet newcomers. Occasionally during the week there would be a knock on the door and we would find a visitor to Caithness, keen to view 'the Lybster Stone.'

When we had first arrived in the parish, we had seen a sign on the front fence of the Lybster church that read. 'Lybster Stone.' At first we had naively assumed that the particular stone from which the fence was constructed was made of a special stone found only around Lybster, in the same way one sees advertisements in Australia for "Gosford Sandstone."

One day, while inspecting the outside of the Church, we saw a rough shelter attached to the eastern wall, and in the shelter we saw a very large stone, with an unusually designed cross cut into it. We were to learn that it is believed the stone came from an ancient monastery that was situated above the harbour about fifteen hundred years ago. It may well have been there when the Vikings arrived, somewhere around the 6th century AD. Experts who have examined the stone believe the cross is of a design used about that time. The stone has a hollowed-out section which, some suggest, may have been used as a baptismal font.

All other evidence concerning the monastery has vanished. Only the 'Lybster Stone' remains.

One Sunday we had visitors at the Dunbeath Kirk which swelled the numbers nicely, but even more visitors at the Lybster Kirk, for there was a baptism there. In fact the family and friends of parents and infant just about filled the Kirk. It was most pleasing to see. During the service, little Tyler was received into the family and household of faith, through baptism.

The parents had invited Janet and me to join them at a celebratory function, but we had other plans afoot, made some weeks before.

One hour and fifteen minutes after the end of the Lybster service, bags in the boot, we were in the car and heading south, down the A99 to the A9 and down to a turn-off just before Dornoch, where we turned right, along a minor road.

It was so marvellous, getting off the major roads. Our journey took us along the side of the lovely Dornoch Firth, but we had only glimpses of it through foliage of deepest green, while here and there patches of lovely mauve wild foxgloves nodded a colourful greeting.

We arrived at the picture-book pretty village of Bonar Bridge where we turned off again, travelling through rolling hills, to arrive eventually at a lovely, secluded little hamlet called Rosehall. It was time for a cuppa – or as the old Caithness folk would say, "a wee cuppie."

Janet went to the boot to get the thermos while I walked along the roadside a little.

I paused on the pretty stone bridge we'd just crossed in the car and looked down on the small river Cassley, burbling and bubbling its gentle way around shaded banks and braes to join, eventually, the great Dornoch Firth on its way to the sea.

It was a scene of quite exquisite beauty; one to sweeten even the most jaded soul.

Walking back along the road I saw some berries peeping through the foxgloves lining the road. When I had a closer look, I discovered they were wild raspberries, ripe and delicious.

The village was so quiet! The only person we saw was a lady walking a West Highland terrier, who exchanged a pleasant word with us.

We sat on a low, lichen covered stone wall, to enjoy our simple repast, then, hunger and thirst satiated, we were on our way again, travelling the rolling green hills, through rain-misted glens, up through steepening hills beside the Strath of Oykel, ever higher, looking down to the valley floor, where the river Oykel lay like a carelessly thrown silver ribbon, past the odd lonely house until we arrived at a picturesque bay, called Ardmair, and we knew then that we were not far from Ullapool.

The bay lies in the shelter of a great, cloud-wreathed peak, and all was grey before the falling rain, but nothing could disguise the beauty of the place.

We paused awhile to drink it all in before heading off again, and soon were on a hill overlooking Ullapool, all misted with rain, where the Hebridean ferry "Isle of Lewis" was nosing into her berth.

Keen to find a B&B, we drove down into the town, for the hour was drawing on, although it was still quite light. We were fortunate enough to strike oil almost at once, at a charming home in a quiet street where a pleasant and rather shy lady who introduced herself as Joan directed us to a comfortable room.

Because it was still light, we decided to have a quick look at the town and then have a meal.

Ullapool is a living picture-postcard. It is old-world picturesque; its white houses and shops set right on the harbour, where fishing boats nestled against the quay and noisy gulls cut the sky on angled wings.

From the street one looks down wide Annat Bay, until sea, sky and hills meet.

The Caledonian hotel, the grandest-looking building in Ullapool, provided a good and tasty repast for a reasonable price.

The following day our B&B hostess provided a very fine breakfast. By 9.00am we had bidden her farewell and were on our way.

With time on our hands we had a look at the various attractions in Ullapool and at last settled for a four-hour cruise to the Summer Isles aboard "Summer Queen", a smallish cruise boat. The Summer Isles – what an enchanting name! It sounded a delightful place to visit.

The day however was overcast and rather chilly, and it was a little difficult to imagine local offshore islands that would be in any way summery, but we were going for the experience, not the temperature.

With about thirty other souls we boarded "Summer Queen" and departed at 10.00am.

Our vessel was quite comfortable and there was plenty of room. We motored down Annat Bay to open water as the weather began to deteriorate and soon "Summer Queen" was punching into choppy seas. We had superb views of the Summer Islands and also back to the towering mountain heights of the mainland.

The passengers kept largely to themselves, but we heard many different languages being spoken and soon fell into conversation with a friendly German girl and her friend.

Her English was very good, his almost non-existent.

The Summer Islands are not exactly spectacular, but we were seeing them in wet and chilly conditions. Only one of the islands is inhabited: the island of Tenera Mhor, where only seven people live.

"Summer Queen" berthed at the small jetty at Tenera Mhor, up which we climbed, to be greeted by a path leading towards a long building with a red phone box outside. This, we had been told, was the local shop and post office, where we could buy postcards and send them on their way with a special Tenera Mhor stamp.

We followed the others along the path, grateful for the warm clothing that protected us from the strong, chilly wind blowing across the island.

The post office building is really a long shed, with a few tables and chairs, while a small café provided simple fare such as sandwiches, cakes, tea, coffee and cold drinks for the visitors who call.

The locals were very charming and welcoming. We bought a couple of postcards and posted them, bearing the special Tenera Mhor stamp.

An hour later we were aboard ship again and heading out around more of the islands, all looking a tad bleak in the weather conditions. "Summer Queen" moved out into open water, where conditions were decidedly rougher. I decided to get a good photograph of the waves, and unwisely moved to the forward deck. I lifted the camera and had it ready for the next wave to hit. I did not have to wait long; nor did I anticipate the size of the wave. A great white wall of water shot up over the bow and completely engulfed me! I fell back before it and just managed to get back to the door into the saloon. I came in, completely drenched.

Janet looked at me in astonishment. "What happened to you? Did you fall overboard?" I certainly looked as if I had and in fact was grateful that the wave did not take me with it when it disappeared over the side.

It was far too wet and wild to venture outside, so we all sat inside. I found myself seated next to a chap and soon engaged him in conversation.

He was, he told me, in somewhat halting English, Spanish, from the north of Spain; that his name was the equivalent of David in English and that he, his wife and two other couples were in three cars, travelling around Scotland. His wife, a dark-eyed, attractive woman, was beside him, and smiled at me from time to time.

"Mya wife," he informed me, "doesa nota spika da word of Eengleesh."

Another man came to speak to David, who introduced us to him. "Dees eess my friend, Manuel," he told me. Manuel could speak excellent English.

"Do you come from Barcelona?" I asked.

No, he told me, he too comes from northern Spain, on the other side of the country from Barcelona. It seems he had not seen "Fawlty Towers" so was unaware of the Manuel of that series, which was probably just as well.

We were still chatting when the "Summer Queen" arrived back at Ullapool.

When we parted, David's wife presented both cheeks to be kissed. "Eetsa da custom eena my contry" explained David. The other Spanish friends waved and smiled farewell. I really enjoyed my too-brief time with those charming people, and as they left I wished that my Spanish was as good as Manuel's English.

After a brief lunch we too bade farewell to lovely Ullapool.

We headed south down the coast road, the A835. Janet was very keen to see a beautiful tree garden, along that section of the road. We didn't have far to go before we arrived. The garden is called Leckmelm Gardens, just three miles from Ullapool. A great high wall protects it from the road. We parked and went in, and at once were taken back centuries. There is acre upon acre of dense forest, of just about every type of tree under the sun. A lot of it is very dense, but it is all beautiful. Janet was utterly captivated and took many photos. Some of the trees are enormous and are obviously centuries old. At one time the garden had been abandoned for about a hundred years, but latterly someone has been restoring it and we saw signs of work being done. I took a photo of Janet among the trees, looking like a wood sprite, while she took one of me in which I resemble a somewhat vacant-looking garden gnome.

Finally we left – we were the only ones exploring – and headed south again, down past the quiet waters of Loch Broom, until we arrived at the turn-off leading to the Corrieshalloch Gorge and Measch Falls.

We parked the car and walked through some forest until we came to the gorge, where an amazing sight met our gaze. The gorge is about two-hundred feet (about 65 metres) deep, in heavily wooded country, and is crossed by a suspension bridge that sways a bit as one crosses.

A warning at the start calls for no more than six people to be on the bridge at any one time.

The gorge, with it tumbling white waterfall, is breathtaking and beautiful, although Corrishalloch means, in the Gaelic, "Ugly hollow."

On the other side is a walk along the edge of the gorge that leads to a platform sticking out into space… not recommended for anyone with vertigo, but the view is glorious.

We walked back to the other side and followed a path for about a mile to the Measch Falls, which is a very high, slender waterfall plunging down into the floor of the gorge and is well worth the walk. That walk of something over a mile brought us eventually back to the car, and on the way there are spectacularly beautiful views all the way down to Loch Broom.

We drove south again, to the charming village of Strathpeffer, then Dingwall and finally Inverness, where we promptly got lost. The traffic was heavy, streets ran off everywhere, and after the quiet beauty of the past couple of days, I felt utterly miserable.

We found a street full of B&Bs but as it turned out, all but one were completely booked out so grabbed the vacant one while we could.

To park the car behind the B&B, I had to drive between two buildings, the space so narrow it was necessary to fold in both driving mirrors and be directed in by the man of the house. There were inches either side – a nerve-wracking experience!

The B&B owners were quite charming and helpful, so when my nerves had settled down we went for a walk. It was no more than a five minute walk to the bridge over the lovely river Ness, on which handsome Inverness castle looks down. Opposite the castle, on the other side of the river, which is the side we were on, is the stately Columba Hotel, so we popped in there for a pleasant meal before returning to our B&B, for we were both tired.

Next morning our cheerful hostess served a delicious and ample meal and gave us directions out of Inverness – which happened to be, had I only known, at the other end of the street.

I had a nightmare that night about getting our car out from between the buildings, but the B&B lady's hubby has been directing cars out for years, and did so this time as well, with no problems.

Finally we were on our way, managing to get lost only once more, but were finally heading in the right direction.

Culloden is only four miles from Inverness, so we decided to pay a visit to the famous but sad battlefield, site of the last major conflict on British soil, in AD 1746.

There is a large and impressive visitors' centre at Culloden.

Entry is not cheap, for it is a charity that receives no government assistance, but it is worth every penny.

We spent ages looking at all the relics from the battle: shields and swords and flintlock rifles and pistols and other items. There is also a film shown that is a graphic re-enactment of the battle itself - definitely not to be recommended to the squeamish.

We then went on a guided tour of the battlefield. We were shown the actual battle lines where the Government Army and the Jacobite Army stood 500 yards apart, facing each other. The Jacobite Army lost, and 1,500 of its men were killed.

We saw the clan burial sites of mass graves, with headstones denoting what clansmen are buried there: McGilvrays and Macintoshes and Camerons and McKays and all the rest.

It was the saddest place, and it is said that for years, no bird would sing there. We noted that all the visitors spoke in hushed tones, even out on the battlefield.

There is too much there to go into detail, but let it be said that Culloden and its history are not to be missed by any who visit Inverness.

A shop there sells all sorts of Culloden books and curios and memorabilia and souvenirs. There was also a little cafe where Janet and I had a bite before heading north, back to beautiful Caithness.

Chapter 35

Mainly about things ancient

Reminding the folk of Latheron parish that there were two active churches in the district, at Dunbeath and Lybster, was for me an important role, and the only way a minister can get to know his church family and interest others is by calling on them, to get to know them and they him. Latheron had been without a minister for nearly ten years and my time, like a north of Scotland summer, was regrettably short.

There were others who had been active in the church community until age overtook them and they could not get about very freely anymore. They certainly needed the visit of a minister.

One of the elderly I called on one day was a delightful lady whose name was Nellie, who lived in one of the villages nearby.

"I've just been tae see the doctor concerning my fleabite-itis," she told me. "He's given me some antibiotics. He's a funny man! He says tae me 'You've a fine pair o' legs on you, Nellie – indeed you have - better than many o' the young things who come in here, hasn't she, nurse?' And nurse agreed! It gave me quite a lift, I can tell you, even if he is an auld flatterer!"

As she made us a cup of tea I asked "Do you have a problem with fleas around here?"

"Och, no! It's my legs! Nothing to do with fleas. They're very painful and the doctor told me I have fleabite-itis."

As we had our cup of tea and cake she asked "I suppose you've been aroond, seeing the wee wiffies?"

Um – what's a wiffy; a wife?"

"You've no heard of it? It's an old word we use up here and means 'old woman' – like me!"

I smiled. "Somehow, Nellie, I don't think you will ever be classed as an old woman, "and that certainly applies to your mind and sense of humour!"

When I got home I asked Janet about fleabite-itis. She'd never heard of it.

"It's something to do with her legs," I told her.

Suddenly Janet said "I'll bet it's phlebitis! "Itis" means inflammation, and phleb is to do with the veins. I'm sure that's what Nellie's 'fleabite-itis is'."

I'm sure she was correct. I recall many older Australians over the years who have told me they are not well – they have "the bronichals" which is bronchitis, or men who tell me that they have prostrate, rather than prostate, problems. When I hear that, I have a sudden, mad vision of the sufferer falling on his face.

Over the weeks I found many others like dear little Nellie whom I'd have loved to call on, again and again, for there was a need, but time was against me.

One day we decided to visit the Camster Cairns; two Neolithic age burial cairns (somewhere around 5,000 years old), about four miles from Lybster along the road to Watten, another village like Lybster.

We had heard so much about the cairns but were waiting for a fine day to go.

Between Lybster and the cairns there is virtually nothing, apart from the odd croft house.

We were really surprised when we got there. The two cairns are sitting just off the road and are quite large and in excellent order. One is called the long cairn and the other, smaller cairn is called the round cairn. The long cairn is about seventy metres long and about twenty metres wide, while the smaller (round) cairn is about twenty metres in diameter.

The particular use the cairns were put to has been lost in the mists of time, but they were burial cairns. One theory is that they were used to bury tribal chiefs. The long cairn, which has two entrances, has a sort of platform at one end where, it is surmised, ceremonies were held – possibly funeral services or, as others suggest, for the worship of a "Mother Earth" goddess.

There is an unlocked gate into each of the cairns so entering them is permitted. I was very unhappy at the thought of entering, but eventually did. Janet came with me.

It is necessary more or less to crawl for the first part along a narrow passageway before one can stand upright.

The Scottish Heritage people have put a skylight in the roof of the main chambers so it is quite light inside. I had an uneasy feeling in there, but Janet did not feel it. I felt like an intruder and left as soon as possible. I would not go into the other entrance of the long cairn or into the round cairn, even although human remains are long gone from either cairn. When I have departed this earthly realm, I would like my mortal remains to be undisturbed for all time, until the last trump sounds.

It was an eerie experience, to my mind, visiting the cairns, but one not to be missed.

I was cheered by another relic near the cairns: an ancient, round sheepfold, built of stone, with a narrow gate across which the shepherd would sleep to guard the sheep from marauding animals, and also prevent the sheep from wandering out. There are still shepherds in Scotland and there were at least two retired shepherds in the Latheron parish.

As I looked at the ancient sheepfold I recalled that the Lord had identified Himself as the Good Shepherd in John chapter 10 and also as the gate: the One Who protects His sheep:

I tell you the truth: I am the gate for the sheep (verse 7) and I am the gate. Whoever enters through Me will be saved. (verse 9).(NIV).

When one visits the cairns and thinks of the ancients who lived and died there, and recalls that the birth of Jesus Himself lay approximately three thousand years into their future, it is a signal reminder of the shortness of human life, and makes very significant the words of Psalm 90:4: For a thousand years in Thy sight are like a day that is past, or a watch in the night. (NIV)

Finally we departed, but the visit to the cairns and the sight of the ancient sheepfold, left a lasting impression on both of us.

Just before we hit the main road on the way home we screeched to a stop – or rather, the car did, after I applied the brakes quite heavily.

I had seen a small creature on the side of the road and at first took it to be a hedgehog, for there were many around the district.

Grabbing the camera, I jumped from the car and ran back down the road. The small creature uncoiled itself and started running away but thankfully, not into the field beside the road. It had a strange flowing gait that reminded me of a ferret. Finally it stopped to stare at me. I stared back. It looked like a ferret in its build, but obviously was not, for instead of a narrow pointed little face it had a round face with little round ears. It paused just long enough for me to get a picture before legging it into the mulga (to use an Australianism).

I was completely puzzled. Had I discovered a new, hitherto unknown species?

Back at the manse, I printed out a copy of the photograph and later took it to the Jabos ("Just A Bunch Of Singers") group, which was practising that evening in the church hall.

They all took one look at it and said in unison, "That's a polecat!"

"You were lucky to get a shot like that," someone said. "They are shy. You see them dead on the road sometimes."

Andrew added, "Our previous dog liked to chase rabbits. He made the mistake of chasing a polecat once. By the time he came back with a bloodied face he'd made a firm resolve never to chase one again!"

Pauline, the session clerk, sang with the Jabos group, had an excellent voice and also played the violin.

I once asked Pauline's husband, John the deacon, if he too had any musical talent.

"Och, no," he replied, with a rueful shake of the head, "I asked the Lord for the gift of music. I think He must have thought I said muesli! What about you – how are you on the didgeridoo?"

I shook my head. "Never tried, but when I was a child I used to play on the linoleum."

We considered our lack of musical talents in silence for a while. "Oh well, never mind, John," I told him at last, "you have many other gifts which you use to the full," and as that Presbytery's very hard working – in fact, overworked and supposedly retired deacon, it was a fact.

The following day we were in Wick, where I decided to get a haircut.

There were two barbers in Wick; both female. I had been to both and discovered them to be first-rate, about the same level in the skill department, so I usually visited them turnabout.

This time I decided it was Jenny's turn. She was a funny girl, in the best sense of the word, for she had a great sense of humour and really enjoyed a chat.

When I walked in, it was to discover that I was the only one in the shop.

She smiled when she saw me enter. "Och, if it's no' the crocodile wrestling parson from Australia! You're in luck, Lachlan. You can sit doon straight away." She remembered me because I was her only Australian customer.

Jenny obviously thought she was not doing her job unless she continued to cut as she talked, so I usually left her shop with only a small thatch of hair.

I was fascinated, listening to her, for she had a very pronounced Caithness accent, and I didn't like to interrupt. A couple of times, as I looked in the mirror, watching my usual crop of thick hair diminishing by the second I said nervously, "That looks fine, Jenny."

"OK," she replied, still snipping, "I'll just give it a wee trim here and a wee trim there." (snip-snip-snip-snip-snip).

Oh well, I thought as I left the shop, very much aware of the nippy Caithness breeze around my ears, I won't need another haircut for months. It was a very good haircut anyway.

In the afternoon we went to Dunbeath Care Centre where we'd been invited, and discovered with some surprise that I was 'on' as the entertainment! It wasn't hard… I talked about Australia, and soon everyone had a story to tell of their own experiences.

I also told them of my part-time jobs as a crocodile wrestler as well as a funnel web spider milker, done to extract the venom from arguably the world's deadliest spider, to make anti-venene. "The spider's teats are so tiny," I told them, "and one has to avoid being fatally bitten at the same time."

The time soon passed, with a lot of hearty laughter all round at my highly unlikely bush yarns. A couple almost believed my crocodile and spider stories…

Later that day we grabbed our walker's sticks that had been made for us by John the shepherd and walked up the hill above Lybster harbour, where the heather bloomed in purple splendour. The summer days meant a long gloaming, as the old Scots called twilight. Darkness was still many hours away.

Our sticks were really handy, for the way up was on a narrow path, somewhat waterlogged with all the recent rain, and the bracken grew to the very edge.

It was so lovely up there among the heather, with not another soul anywhere, and above us a great wide Caithness sky, for the rain had cleared.

Despite my walker's stick I did manage to fall once when I accidentally stepped into a ditch hidden in the bracken and ended up with my 'ooter in the 'eather, much to Janet's amusement.

"While we're here," Janet said, "Let's try to find the Brethren Well." We had been told that somewhere on the hill there was a mysterious well of ancient origin, known as The Brethren Well, and we'd even been given vague directions.

We searched around the general area on the hill and at last spotted it, nearly hidden among the bracken, peat and heather. The well itself was long gone, but the spring that fed it still bubbled up. We knelt to read the fascinating history inscribed on a plaque above it.

According to the plaque, the well was probably built and used by an order of monks who lived nearby in a monastery, somewhere around the 6th century AD. There is now no longer any sign of the monastery, but it is believed it was there when the Norsemen arrived, for Lybster was known to the Vikings as Halligoe: The Sacred Inlet.

According to ancient legend, the water is supposed to have healing properties, but it didn't look too clean to us.

"Oh well," I told Janet, "I'll give it a try. I've had to drink a lot worse than this from waterholes and billabongs in Australia over the years."

I scooped up some of the water and drank it. It was fresh, and I had an odd, irrational sensation of being connected somehow through the water to the ancient monks who had used the water from the well fifteen centuries before me.

It was on this site that a large stone (about one metre long) was found with a cross engraved on it, which is now known as "The Lybster Stone, situated in the grounds of the Lybster Kirk.

After the monks disappeared (no one knows when), the well was in continual use by crofting families right up until 1955, making it probably the most ancient continually used well in the world.

On the way down the path we saw a black and white flash, and not long after, Ben, a border collie we know appeared, stick in mouth.

Down a bit further we met the collie's owners, so chatted for a while, throwing the stick occasionally to an ever-waiting Ben.

From there we made our way down the path to the tiny harbour for a cappuccino at 'Waterlines,' the heritage museum run by the locals, which has a little cafeteria attached.

Just offshore we saw a fishing boat making its way in against a rising sea, for the wind was picking up again.

Chapter 36

Stroma

One Monday morning in late June we set off for John o' Groats, from where we intended to visit the deserted island of Stroma. Of course it was at Janet's initiative. Had it not been for her, I would have just kept on working. She was the one who had ideas of what to see.

We had been fascinated by Stroma when first we'd seen it from the road, at the top of a hill as we approached John o' Groats; a small island, two miles offshore. We could see what looked like grey houses on the island, and wondered about its inhabitants. Only later were we to learn that the island is deserted, the houses empty; an island given over to the many sheep that roam there.

The name Stroma is Norse, dating from the time of the Viking rule, which ended a thousand years ago. We knew from our time in Shetland, that an 'a' on the end of a Norse word can mean 'small island.' 'Strom' means 'stream' and the 'a' on the end indicates 'island' so Stroma means, literally, 'small island in the stream.'

The 'stream' is the wild waters of Pentland Firth, among the most dangerous anywhere, stretching up to the Orkneys.

We decided to take our time getting to John o' Groats, for we were in no hurry, so turned off at the little village of Thrumster, half way to Wick, to visit the Yarrows, with its lovely loch, (the Loch of Yarrows) and its archaeological trail, where we walked to the ruin of a broch (fort) approximately two thousand years old. Apart from the odd croft, it is lonely country.

"I wonder what 'Yarrows' means?" I asked Janet as we headed back to Thrumster and the road north.

"I have an idea a yarrow is a fragrant sort of a herb," Janet told me, "so the 'loch of yarrows' must be surrounded in yarrows." She is very keen on gardening and knows a lot about flowers and plants and things. In fact at risk of repeating myself, my ignorance of plant life is such that it was quite late in life before I discovered that 'diphtheria' is not a flower, but some sort of ailment. I used to speak of it glibly, when visiting, and noting a vase of flowers the hostess had on the table would comment "They're lovely! Are they diphtherias?"

"No – they're geraniums." (accompanied by odd look).

When we arrived at John o' Groats we were still early, so travelled the short distance to see the stacks at Duncansby Head – three huge, pointed rocks standing in the sea, two of which look like witches' hats. The cliffs are very high, and dangerous.

At Duncansby Head there are a couple of narrow inlets, with great drops into the sea below – what we Caithness locals (and Shetlanders) call Geos. Geo is a Gaelic word, meaning "cove."

The gulls were still nesting and I managed to get a beautiful picture of nesting gulls, with their nest built into the cliffs, with lovely wildflowers surrounding them. I was captivated by the scene.

Finally, we went down to John o' Groats, where by the harbour we found the office of one of the two businesses that operated vessels out to Stroma on sight-seeing tours.

"Ours is a smallish boat," the operator told us; "in fact it's what is known as a RIB, or Rigid Inflatable Boat. It's open, so you will see a lot, and has shallow draft, so we can duck in anywhere and we'll be exploring some of the caves. The boat will seat twelve, but only four passengers have booked. There are two crew members. Now because the Pentland Firth is one of the most dangerous waterways in the world, suitable precautions have to be taken so you will be fitted out with oilskins and lifejackets."

The other two were a couple of English folk. Fortunately, the day was superb – sunny and windless, and the Pentland Firth like a millpond.

There were two crew on board who were attentive and helpful.

We motored over to the island which did not take long. When we got there we could see what appeared to be a chapel but in fact it is a mausoleum, filled with the ancient dead, all of them Kennedys. The Kennedy clan owned the island for centuries we were told.

The mausoleum is situated in the walled cemetery.

What followed is hard to describe, for it was a magic journey as far as Janet and I are concerned.

The inflatable, with such shallow draft, could nudge in among the rocks right by the shoreline. We were treated to a moving panorama of (mainly) birdlife, including puffins on the water and on the hills.

The birds largely ignored us. We motored slowly into strange sea-caves, some huge.

Above us in one cave were veritable galleries of seabirds, row upon row, almost as if they were waiting for some marvellous opera of the sea to start, and I thought at once of Bizet's "The Pearl Fishers" and could almost hear, in the ripple of the water, the song from that opera In the Depths of the Temple.

Deep in one cave we found a family of seals enjoying the solitude and silence, and I thought of Matthew Arnold's beautiful poem, "The Forsaken Merman" and his words:

"Sea green caverns, cool and deep, where the winds are all asleep..."

In one cave, we were told, there was, a century or so ago, a whisky still which the excise men (customs) never found. It is called "Smugglers' Cave." I was fascinated and recall many great yarns of my youth, including "Captain Clegg" who was a pious clergyman by day and the chief of the smugglers by night.

Out we went around the top end of the island where there is a lighthouse. Our crewman pointed out a line of very disturbed water. "That is the edge of a giant whirlpool called The Swilkie" he told us. "In rough weather there can be a wall of water ten metres high and four hundred metres across. It's very dangerous and has claimed many a ship."

Just before, we had passed the rusted remains of a ship hard up against the rocks.

We moved on, and suddenly were passing along the edge of more very rough water. The crewman pointed. "The witches' cauldron" he told us; "which is a giant whirlpool. There is a huge hole in the seafloor. The sea pours in and is thrown out, and more water rushes in. Get caught in that, and you go down into it." I prayed those engines to keep going.

Away from us there was a line of white water that stretches up to the Orkneys, called "The Merry Men of Mey." It's where the North Sea and the Atlantic meet and its wild turbulent waters, its rushing currents and tides have proved fatal to many a brave sailorman.

All the waters of Pentland Firth are very dangerous.

Our boat moved to the other side of the island, then back to John o' Groats.

What an adventure – one I'll never forget. It is one I'd love to do again.

Chapter 37

Samantha

"Lachlan," said Rhona as she passed me a plate of her tasty shortbread, "if you're still looking for people to visit who have not seen a minister for a long time, I have another name for you."

Rhona was one of the elders who lived at the Dunbeath end of the parish, and I was on my pastoral rounds.

"Are there any problems?" I asked as I selected one of Rhona's culinary masterpieces.

"Well, yes. Dugald Lamond and his wife Mary are getting on in age a wee bit. Dugald would be in his early nineties and has terminal cancer, and I've been told he has dementia. His time is short. Mary is not much younger but her health is good. Fortunately, they have two adult children who live around here. They also have a relative in Inverness who is a minister and he will officiate when the time comes. He can't be here as often as he would like, for he has a parish to run. I know the old couple would appreciate a visit. They live at the very end of High Bluff road."

I knew the road. It was well out to the west of Dunbeath, and petered out from narrow but sealed, to narrow unsealed.

I'd never been out as far as the end but decided to go the following day.

Just before 10.00am the next day I turned off the main road south of Dunbeath and headed west for a few miles along an almost deserted road, until a faded signpost pointed me to High Bluff Road. I followed it until it ended abruptly at a croft gate from which hung a rough, hand-written sign: "Dugald Lamond." I had arrived.

The Lamond croft house was similar to so many in the district: grey stone, two-storey with a chimney at either end. It was made for cold weather. A couple of cars were parked in the drive.

My knock at the door was answered by a pleasant-faced, dark-headed, plumpish woman, somewhere in her fifties, I guessed. She looked at me enquiringly.

I introduced myself and said "I believe Mr Lamond is not at all well, so thought I'd drop in to see how he is."

She smiled. "Come in, Mr Ness – I'm Jeanette Lamond, Mr and Mrs Lamond's daughter."

As we started down the hall towards the sitting room, she stopped. "You've arrived when there's a wee bit of dissension going on. I'll put you quickly in the picture." Her voice was low. "Basically, my father has 'lost it.' He's 93, and has cancer as well as dementia, but my mother can't seem to come to terms with his dementia. She thinks he's as well, mentally, as ever he was. As far as she's concerned, anything he says, goes. It's all over a cat, would you believe? He's had his cat, Samantha, for about five years, ever since it was a kitten. He loves it, and says that when he dies, he wants the cat put to sleep and buried with him. My mother is happy about it, for she hates cats. My brother Graeme is indifferent to cats so is sitting on the fence, as they say, while I hate the very thought of it."

As she spoke, a shiver of horror ran down my spine. How, I wondered, could anyone consider killing a perfectly healthy young cat for such a reason? It was bizarre.

Jeanette showed me into the room and introduced me. They all smiled, nodded to me and murmured polite words of welcome, but I could see I'd interrupted something. Seated by the fire on a settee was the old man, Dugald Lamond, in pyjamas, dressing gown and slippers, thin as a tin whistle with wispy grey hair, his white bristly chin indicating the need of a shave. Beside him was his wife Mary, small and plump and lined, her white hair pulled back in a severe bun. She looked tense. On the other side of the fire sat Jeanette's brother, tall and dark-headed who, like his sister, appeared to be somewhere in his fifties. He had stood when Jeanette introduced me and smiled cordially, but I could sense tension in the room.

The old man nodded to me. "Good morning, minister - Jeanette - fetch the minister a cup of tea." He pointed to a vacant chair. "Sit down, please." He began to cough wheezily. Jeanette handed me the tea. I sipped it nervously, for the tension in the room had unsettled me.

"I'm pleased to meet you," I began as I took the seat. "Rhona at Dunbeath mentioned…"

"Are you American?" broke in Mr Lamond.

"No – Australian. I'm here for a few months -"

"Who told you about us?" wheezed Mr Lamond.

"It was Rhona, at Dunbeath -"

"Are you American?" interrupted Mr Lamond again.

The difficulty of the situation and the extent of Mr Lamond's dementia began to dawn on me.

"Dad, Mr Ness came all the way here just to see how you are," said Jeanette gently. "Would you like to go for a little walk in the garden?"

"Yes, yes, that would be nice," mumbled the old man as his daughter helped him to his feet.

I was impressed. Jeanette knew the technique of diverting the attention of dementia sufferers.

As they left the room, a black cat strolled in, obviously very much at home. This, I thought, must be Samantha. She seemed to realise that there was a stranger in the room, for she walked to me and sniffed my trouser-leg curiously before jumping onto my lap for further investigation. I noted that her eyes were an unusually deep green. The little black cat with the bright green eyes… the words of an old poem floated into to my mind. I stroked her and could hear her rumbling purr. She was completely black, apart from a tiny area of white, the size of my little fingernail, on her right front leg.

Graeme and his mother watched me in silence. "That's dad's cat, Samantha, Mr Ness," Graeme ventured, "and I see you found the only white patch on her."

"I suppose it's a sort of feline birthmark?" I suggested.

"Not at all," Graeme replied. "The cat had to have an injection at one time. The Vet shaved that spot to insert the needle, and when the fur grew back, it was completely white."

"I suppose Samantha will be a faithful little companion for you in time, Mrs Lamond" I suggested, hoping to plant an idea in the elderly lady's mind.

"It won't be!" she snapped. "I don't care what anyone says. When Dugald dies, that cat is going into the grave with him. That's what Dugald wants, and I couldn't bear having the animal around the place after he's gone. I can't stand it – slinky thing that it is!"

Years of experience as well as a useful dose of common sense warned me against the folly of becoming emotionally involved in family squabbles – I'd seen disastrous consequences before. The thought of the beautiful animal being put down for such a bizarre reason however, sickened me, but apart from a miracle, Samantha's prospects were not rosy.

I changed the subject. "Is your husband very ill, Mrs Lamond?"

"Aye – very sick. The cancer has him, in the lungs. Never smoked in his life, you know. He'll be lucky to see out the week."

When I left, I knew a little more. Graeme lived with his wife Myra and two teenage children on the other side of Wick. Jeanette was a widow. She had a profitable online business and worked from her home near Berriedale, a small village south of Dunbeath.

In the following couple of weeks I called a number of times on Dugald and his wife to gauge how things were going for them. It was obvious the old man was sinking fast, but Mrs Lamond refused to have him put in hospital. She would, she said, nurse him to the end, as she'd nursed her parents, and his.

Each time I visited, Samantha, purring contentedly, came to greet me, and then jump onto my lap to check me out with those deep, sea-green eyes.

On my last visit, Mr Lamond was sleeping heavily on the settee. "He's on pain-killing drugs now," his wife said. "They say the cancer is in his bones as well."

"Who's going to... to take Samantha to the Vet when the time comes, Mrs Lamond?"

"Jeanette. I asked her. She's the closest, and there's a veterinary clinic down her way."

The following day I called in on Jeanette. She had a pleasant cottage in a quiet little street, and I felt concerned for her. I knew she felt the same revulsion I did at the thought of little Samantha's fate.

Jeanette showed me through to the sitting room. "Find a seat, Lachlan, while I make a pot of tea."

"Hullo – I didn't know you had a cat too, Jeanette!" I exclaimed. On a chair was a snow-white cat, apparently asleep.

"Pick her up if you like, Lachlan," Jeanette called. "She won't mind. She's very agreeable."

I walked to the chair and put my hand on the sleeping form. Something didn't seem right. It appeared to be stiff, and dead.

I picked it up – and realisation dawned. It wasn't a real cat at all, but a cat-sized toy, made to look like the real thing. I turned and saw Jeanette watching me from the door, smiling.

"I'm sorry, Lachlan – I just had to watch! That creature has fooled so many! Pull its tail."

I pulled, and the 'cat' hissed.

"Stroke it." I did so. A cat-like purr rumbled from somewhere inside.

"Now squeeze it." I did, and was rewarded with an impressively realistic "Miaow!"

I turned it to look into its glass eyes. I could have been looking at a real cat. "It's so lifelike, Jeanette! Where did you get it?"

"In Aberdeen. I was down there to pick up some supplies for my business a few months ago, and saw it in a shop. I couldn't resist it. I call her Petra. It's Greek for 'rock.' She has no real heart."

"I take it you like cats."

"I do. I'll get another cat, one of these days. My dear little tabby, Agatha, died about a year ago, and I haven't tried to get another. Even thinking about a replacement makes me feel sad."

Quite a few of the homes I'd visited had life-sized toy dogs, mainly border collies sitting in easy chairs, looking surprisingly real, but Jeanette's was the first 'cat' I'd seen.

A week later, Rhona rang. "Mr Dugald died early this morning, Lachlan. The relative who'll be officiating can't get up from Inverness until tomorrow. I thought you'd like to know."

I went at once. Mrs Lamond was being comforted by Graeme's wife and other relatives, as Graeme stood by awkwardly. I sidled over to him. "I'm very sorry to learn of your father's death, Graeme, even if we all knew it wasn't far off. How are you?"

"I'm coping well enough, and Mum's dealing with it as only she could."

Where's Jeanette?" I asked.

"At the Vet's," he replied. "She took Samantha away about an hour ago. Mum wanted the cat gone as soon as dad died."

When I left, having spent an hour with Mrs Lamond and her family, I felt sick at heart. I knew I could not have done what Jeanette had been forced to do.

The funeral was held in one of the Wick churches towards the end of the week. I was there early. The coffin-lid was back far enough to reveal the old man's face and chest, and as I looked down on the crofter's mortal remains I could see one black feline ear, just visible; the rest of the little animal tucked in very close. A minute later the funeral director closed the lid forever.

Among the mourners I saw Jeanette, sitting with some other family members, and it was obvious she'd been crying. She saw me and gave a tearful smile.

I sat at the back of the church and left immediately after the service. It wasn't 'my' service, in the officiating sense, and the minister was a family member. Best to leave it all to him.

I decided to leave it for a few days before calling on the Lamonds. I rang Graeme, who told me that his mother had been persuaded to spend a few days with family down in Inverness, so I decided to call in on Jeanette the next time I was down her way, which was a few days later.

When Jeanette met me at the door, she appeared to have made a good recovery, for she greeted me brightly. "Make your way into the sitting room, Lachlan – I'll make a pot of tea."

I walked to the sitting room – and stopped at the door. Sleeping on a chair was a cat, but instead of white, it was jet-black.

I went to the kitchen, where Jeanette was pouring water into a teapot. "Did you get a cat after all, Jeanette; or did you dye the little toy Petra?"

"Correct - on both counts!" was Jeanette's enigmatic answer.

I turned to the sitting room – and was greeted by the sight of a very much alive cat, her deep green eyes watching me. She jumped off the chair and walked over, purring, and as she brushed against my leg, I realised she knew me.

I picked her up, and my eyes went to her right front leg. There was a tiny patch of white there.

"What a remarkable coincidence, Jeanette," I called. "This cat has an identical white mark on the same leg, and the same place, that Samantha had."

"Really?" Jeanette's attempt at surprise was not convincing.

"Yes – and she has the same, unusually deep green eyes that Samantha had."

"What a coincidence!" Jeanette's tone was all innocence.

"So what happened to Petra the fake cat, Jeanette? Am I to understand that you dyed it? It didn't happen to be black dye, did it?"

"It's probably best if you don't ask too many questions, Lachlan," Jeanette suggested, smiling, as she handed me my tea.

"Well, OK. So what's the name of your beautiful new cat?

"Anastasia."

"That's unusual."

"Yes, it is. It's a Greek name. It means 'resurrection.'"

Chapter 38

Orkney

Over a period of a couple of months we were delighted to welcome a number of visitors, mostly friends from Australia. In fact the only non-Australian friend was a two-day visit by Lis, who came over from Shetland, where I'd had a parish in the North Isles the previous year (see A Kangaroo Loose in Shetland by Lachlan Ness: www.akangarooloose. com). Most visits were comparatively short, for our visitors were in Britain for some other reason and came up to Caithness just to see us, so we felt very privileged.

During their stays we showed them as much as possible of the picturesque and lovely county of Caithness. Not many had been so far north, despite previous visits to Scotland. We took them to the mysterious stones of Achanavich, as well as Dunnet Head, the most northerly point of mainland Scotland, and of course to the famous John o' Groats, the most northerly town in mainland Scotland.

All of our visitors were keen to visit the Castle of Mey, owned previously by the Queen Mother, which she bequeathed to Prince Charles. Upon her death he turned it into a trust, run locally, to be kept just as it was when his grandmother owned it. Now it is open to visitors for most of the year, apart from those times when Charles is in residence. It is situated on many acres of land, where stock are run and vegetables grown. Souvenirs are sold at the castle; and woollen ties, made from wool spun from the castle's sheep and featuring the castle of Mey tartan, are available. All the money raised is used to help defray the cost of maintaining the castle, which was in a state of disrepair when the Queen Mother bought it with her own money. Now, part of Scotland's history is pristine once again and the trust Prince Charles established will ensure that it remains so.

There are many wonderful stories told of the love the people of Caithness had for the Queen Mother, who fitted in as one of the locals and was often to be seen in her wellies and favourite blue coat, for she loved gardening. Now Charles, through many deeds of kindness and generosity, has also gained the respect and admiration of the local people

Two of our visitors were Sandy and Lyn, who were keen to visit not only us, but to continue northward to the Orkneys, the islands that lie just north of mainland Scotland. The most southerly island lies within sight of the north-east coast, across the Pentland Firth from John o' Groats, only an hour away by one of the Orkney ferries.

It sounds an easy trip – but that stretch of water, known as Pentland Firth, where the North Sea and the Atlantic Ocean converge, can be an extremely rough and highly dangerous waterway, for huge currents meet there. Many ships have gone down around there and many a good sailorman lost, including a number of Caithness deep sea fishermen.

Sandy and Lyn were keen for us to accompany them. I knew that my time there would have to be short because of parish commitments, but one Monday Janet and I and Lyn and Sandy headed seawards from Gills Bay aboard the vehicular ferry Pentalina out into the Pentland Firth which, thankfully, was like a millpond.

Also aboard was Lyn's and Sandy's delightful little rented Peugeot 207: small, very economical but with a surprising amount of room in its comfortable interior.

An hour later we disembarked at the pretty port town of St Margaret's Hope, Orkney.

We drove north through green countryside on a pleasant, winding road along the shore of mighty Scapa Flow, which is a huge inlet. Orkney is awash with history, going back over 5,000 years.

In 1919, at the end of the First World War, there were 74 captured German warships anchored in Scapa Flow under the command of the German Admiral, Von Reuter. The admiral sent out a secret signal to the fleet and at an appointed time, the crews pulled the plugs (sea cocks) in their ships and scuttled every single one of them, and every captured German ship went to the bottom, although none of the crews died.

There is a much more tragic story surrounding Scapa Flow. In October 1939, six weeks after the Second World War commenced, a German U-boat sneaked into Scapa Flow and torpedoed the Royal Navy battleship "Royal Oak" which was at anchor, and 883 officers and men went down with her.

There was so much to see in the brief time we were in Orkney and that's what we did – we went sight-seeing. The capital of Orkney is Kirkwall, a harbour town. In many ways it is similar to Lerwick, the capital of Shetland. It too is quaint and pretty, with a similar-sized population. It is ancient, and the narrow little streets meander everywhere. Amazingly, cars drive down them. We all fell in love with Kirkwall.

We booked into a nice little B&B, run by a pleasant lady with a pronounced Orkney accent. The Orkney accent is very noticeable – it has a sort of sing-song quality.

With only the following day to get in most of the sight-seeing, we set off after booking into the B&B and drove to the harbour town of Stromness, which lies to the west of Kirkwall. It is very similar to Kirkwall both in size and quaintness. We loved Stromness too. The towns and villages of Orkney are unlike anything one would ever encounter in Australia.

We quickly discovered that Orkney appears to be universally green, and very beautiful, with some added qualities. Lyn and I quickly became addicted to the fabled Orkney ice-cream.

On the way back to the B&B we visited Maes Howe, a 5000 year-old chambered cairn (tomb), with a ten-metre tunnel one must crawl along to gain entrance, but it is huge inside.

The following day we were up early and went first to St Magnus's Cathedral, which now belongs to the Church of Scotland. It is awe-inspiring, and was built in 1137. Its founder, Magnus, was murdered and his remains are interred in one of the cathedral's huge pillars.

There is a lovely aura of peace and tranquillity in the cathedral. We could have spent hours there, looking at ancient tombstones, photos, the beautiful furniture including a glorious pulpit, and many other fascinating relics.

Leaving the cathedral, we drove to the "Stones of Stenness" – huge standing stones put there by the ancients for reasons unknown, and then drove on to the amazing "ring of Brodgar" which are more standing stones, forming a giant circle. The stones of Stenness and the Ring of Brodgar have stood there for 5,000 years.

We went from there to the fabled Skara Brae. Apart from roofs, it is an intact Neolithic village, built of stone. Its inhabitants lived there between 3,000BC and 2,500BC. Until the middle of the 19th century no one knew the village was there, but a huge storm uncovered a part of it, so it was excavated. Even the original stone box beds are there. Mystery surrounds the reason why the inhabitants appear to have departed so suddenly, leaving almost everything intact.

About a five minute walk from there is a 17th century manor house called Skaill house. Skaill is the Old Norse name for a hall. One must remember that the Vikings ruled Shetland, Orkney and the north-east of Scotland (including Caithness) for about 500 years. Skaill House is a fascinating place and is full of amazing artefacts, including a dinner service once owned by Captain Cook.

Next day, with some reluctance, we booked out of the B&B and drove back towards St Margaret's Hope, down the coast of the beautiful Scapa Flow.

On the way we stopped to have a look through the lovely and famous Italian Chapel. It was built by Italian prisoners of war in 1943 from two Nissan huts donated by the camp commandant and has been kept in perfect condition ever since. Of course it is Roman Catholic and all the interior is done in the ornate Latin style.

At 12.00 we were aboard Pentalina again and heading south to Gills Bay, mainland Scotland, through, thankfully, calm seas.

Our other Australian guests came and departed in orderly procession: Paul and Mae, Jim and Margaret, Arthur and Joan, then Sandra, then Alan and Pat.

Alan and Pat were bound for the Western Isles when they left us, then on down south to Edinburgh and places further south before returning to Australia.

At breakfast the day before they were due to leave us, Pat said, "Alan and I have just discovered an unfortunate miscalculation in our itinerary. We were supposed to be going to the Edinburgh Tattoo in August, but have discovered we can't fit it in – we even have tickets.

Would you two be interested in them? If you are, they're a gift from us."

Would we ever! When Alan and Pat drove off the next morning, two tickets to the Edinburgh Tattoo were in Janet's bag. We couldn't thank them enough.

Chapter 39

Halcyon days

In a parish that has been without a minister for a long time, getting out and about to meet the folk is especially important and a task I took seriously.

Almost always, I was welcomed warmly. At one home I was greeted by five children and three dogs that came charging down the drive. It was so funny, with the children accompanying me up to the house, chatting away happily while the dogs leaped around, barking in a frenzy of excitement, trying to outdo one another as a welcoming committee.

At another croft there was a large picture of two savage-looking dogs attached to the front gate with a warning: "It will take you ten seconds to run from the house to the gate. We can do it in three." I decided not to visit that day.

"Anyway," I told myself, "I couldn't see anyone around, so the family must be out." I knew it was an excuse.

It was wonderful to be out among those glorious hills, along narrow winding roads that were mostly empty. The sun beamed down mildly from a soft, pale blue sky, upon which the Master Painter had daubed the occasional touch of white. The green and gentle hills were dotted here and there with sheep and shaggy highland cattle, while off to the east the darker blue of the North Sea sparkled and danced.

The tranquil beauty of it all refreshed heart and soul. There is an enchantment about Caithness that is very special and quite spiritual.

It would be interesting, I thought, to be here in the harsher season of winter, when days are short and nights are long, when snows flurry and whirl in the biting winds, and all appears dead and drear . . . and yet, as the Lord said to those who gathered at the apparent deathbed of Jairus's little daughter, "She is not dead, but asleep." Luke 8:52. (NIV). And so she was, and so we rejoice in the miracle of the seasons.

The way we were being quickly drawn into our new life came home to us suddenly one day. Janet was writing a postcard to Australia when she looked up, brow creased. "Can you remember our postcode?"

"KW3 6BN" I told her.

"No – our Australian postcode."

I was still thinking about it when she found it.

"We live on Watson Road, don't we – or is it street?"

"It's road," I told her, "and Watson? That doesn't sound right. That's the name of Andrew's and Jean's whippet."

It took quite a while before we both remembered it – together.

"I just hope we can remember what town we live in when we go back to Oz," I grumbled.

Earlier that day we'd gone for a walk along the strath of Dunbeath. It was a glorious morning, and there was a quality of magic along the strath. It had become a favourite walk of ours when I didn't have a great deal of time off, for it could be covered in an hour or two.

We'd first discovered the strath in April, when we walked down past a former mill. The strath starts just beyond it.

We'd set off down a well-defined path with a rippling burn on one side and quiet woods on the other. A short distance along, we'd entered another world. The music of the waters accompanied the singing of the birds and were the only sounds. There'd been a light haar (mist) which had not completely lifted and the soft haze added an air of mystery.

We journeyed along by the gentle stream, with the palest blue of sky above, through trees adorned in dresses of spring finery. Sprinklings of lovely primroses peeked at us from quiet banks, and new gorse smiled a golden welcome. Our journey took us across two suspension bridges and further along to the ruins of an old building. "You'll see an old building if you walk far enough down the strath," someone had told us; "there used to be a road of sorts there a hundred or so years ago, and that old building was a wayside inn."

That had been months ago. Now it was summer, and we'd learned there was yet more to see along the Strath of Dunbeath.

"Keep an eye out for roe deer," someone else advised. "The deer live in the woods, but they're small, and very shy. You'd be lucky to see one."

We walked and walked, seemingly alone, by woods and little glens and the rippling burn, keeping an eye out for the shy roe deer, but they must have heard us coming. Now and then I stopped, staring, thinking I could see one, but the deer are small, quick, elusive, and the woodland shadows dark and deceptive. "It's easy to see how stories arise of people being beguiled by fairies," I thought to myself; "I think I can sense one, fluttering around me, right now!" I looked. It was a butterfly.

This time we walked further, past the ruin of the inn, past the ancient wall where a monastery once stood a thousand years and more ago, on past burial cairns dating back 5,000 years.

At last we saw it in the distance - the gorge known in the Gaelic as Creag an Fhithich. In English, it means "Prisoner's Leap Gorge."

As we drew closer we could see a sort of natural rock platform, extending out beyond one wall of the gorge. With a lot of effort, we made it to the top and stood on the rocky platform, but it was a long way to the other side. I looked down into the abyss and gave a little shudder.

We'd been told an interesting story connected to the gorge which explains its unusual name, and we were keen to see it.

Centuries ago, the story goes, during the days of the clan wars, Ian MacCormack Gunn was captured by an enemy clan, the Keiths. He was taken to the top of the gorge and told that if he could leap to the other side, he'd be free. If he refused, he'd die at the hands of the Keiths. Either way, the Keiths believed, their prisoner would die. As I looked to the other side of the gorge I could not see how anyone could possibly leap across it. To fall short would be to fall to one's death. The young Gunn agreed to attempt the jump, and before the astonished eyes of his enemies, succeeded. One can only surmise that a combination of fear and adrenalin spurred his effort. The Keiths put out the story that Ian Gunn was an orphan and had been raised on hind's milk, which accounted for his strength.

On the way home I turned off along the Forse Road which heads off towards the sea, for I had been told of the ruin of a castle there. Few ever go there.

We drove as far as we could, parked the car and walked another half mile or so to the cliffs, where we could see the ruin. It must have been an inspiring sight, fifteen centuries ago when it was built, but now only one sad wall remains. The castle was built out on a headland and the only way to the castle wall itself was along a very narrow spit of land which falls away quickly into the sea below. It must have been easily defended, pre-gunpowder.

As we looked out to sea, we saw an oil rig on the horizon, and the incongruity struck us –the ruin of a 6th century castle within sight of a modern oil rig.

A look at a clan map of Scotland shows that Caithness was Gunn and Sinclair clan territory and to this day the clans are well represented.

One Saturday we went off to Sinclair castle, outside Wick right on the coast.

It was a special day for the House of Sinclair, for it was open day at the old 14th century castle. It's a ruin, but the work is progressing to restore a great deal of it.

A heavy haar had settled on the land and it was all white and mysterious, for it is a lonely place. When we got there, a couple of workmen were doing some maintenance, for the Scottish heritage people are keen to stop any further deterioration. We took a few photos as we chatted to the workmen and then the boss asked "Would you like to come in and have a look around?" We jumped at the chance.

He showed us various rooms, and told us how they would have looked in days of yore, for they would have been plastered, possibly wall-papered too. It was a huge castle in its day, this ancestral home of the clan Sinclair, dating back to 1397. At one time, we were told, it would have had a staff of 250. We saw the ancient bread-making oven, and the kitchen, and where the family lived, and even where the toilets were – a small room with a hole disappearing doon to the sea below, for the castle is built on the very edge of a cliff.

Our guide was passionate about the castle's restoration and it is arguably superior to Urquhart Castle on Loch Ness. We spent some time there, fascinated by the castle's former grandeur, before heading off half a mile or so along a path across the fields.

As we walked we admired the new heather, spreading its lovely purple raiment among the grasses and peat. By the middle of the month its beauty would transform many a dark hill and mountain, and brighten the shore of many a lonely loch. Our walk took us to the Sinclair Centre. It is a lighthouse, still in operation, but the clan owns it, and its reading rooms contain much of the clan history.

In the grounds, a carnival atmosphere prevailed. Musicians in mediaeval garb played mediaeval music on mediaeval instruments. There was a stall selling the fabled pure Caithness honey from the nectar of wildflowers. Pipers played merrily, while another man turned wood, and someone else made wooden cart wheels, as they were made centuries ago.

The highlight of the day, however, was yet to come: a re-enactment of a skirmish between English redcoats and highland clansmen! When I enquired if it represented any particular battle, I was told no – it's just something that might have happened in the highlands in the 18th century.

In a clearing in the grounds, the 'battle' finally took place. It was amazingly realistic. Both sides used flintlock rifles, and both sides were appropriately dressed. The enemies faced each other. The redcoat commander issued orders. The redcoats fired, with noisy discharging of weapons and much smoke from black powder.

The highlanders fired back. Men on both sides fell. Then the highlanders charged, in the style that carried their enemy before them in many a conflict. The onlookers cheered as the redcoats fell back in the hand to hand fighting. At last it was over.

The English 'dead' lay thick upon the field, and prisoners were carted off as the onlookers cheered the triumphant highlanders. It was all a lot of fun. There would have been hell to pay up there in the Highlands if the redcoats had won!

The Combined Parish Family Service at Dunbeath the following day went very well indeed, and there was a large congregation. The service was arranged to suit the younger folk, so we sang some jolly Christian songs and enjoyed the bright, joyful atmosphere.

During the service I asked one of the children a question and had to get her to repeat the answer THREE times – I just could not understand her Caithness accent!

Chapter 40

Highland Games

"I don't know if you know," Kevin said as he impaled a chip with his fork from among his plate of fish and chips, "that the Halkirk Highland Games will be held next Saturday. If you don't have anything else on, it should be well worth a visit."

My bearded friend and fellow Australian Presbyterian minister Kevin (also known as Kev the Rev – see the prologue) was doing a locum ministry at St Peter's, a lovely Church of Scotland church in the town of Thurso. Back in Australia several months previously he had lined up the locum work at St Peter's for himself and had shown me a list of vacant parishes in Caithness. It was from that list that I had been able to make contact with Pauline the session clerk in the parish of Latheron, with happy results; at least for me. I hoped and prayed the congregation was not too disappointed.

Thurso, like most of Caithness, including Wick, has its roots back in a Viking past. The name 'Thurso' means, in the Norse, Thor's River, named after the Norse god of thunder, rain and farming, and indeed a large and pleasant river runs by the town.

Kevin and his wife Jenny had a fine manse in the town, and occasionally we had been able to visit each other. St Peter's had a large congregation which kept Kevin very busy, but he loved it.

On that particular day we had made arrangements to catch up with them for lunch at "Horizons," a café in the magnificent Thurso museum, where we'd met on other visits.

Earlier, the four of us had watched a DVD at the museum, titled "Caithness" in which all the scenic beauty of the county through the seasons was beautifully filmed. Copies were available for sale, so we bought one for £8.00. A number of the places featured on the DVD were right on our doorstep around Latheron parish.

Back home, a look at the diary revealed nothing for the following Saturday, so we decided to go to the Halkirk Highland Games. We had been to Halkirk before; a village situated between Wick and Thurso. It is a quiet, pretty village which has a fine river running by one end of town, and each year in the trout fishing season, the village is inundated with keen anglers, for the river has a fine reputation regarding the numbers and size of its trout.

Saturday dawned bright and clear as we set off. Halkirk is not a long drive from Lybster, so we arrived in plenty of time and decided to have a cup of coffee in the hotel by the river, not far from where the games were to be held. The hotel was old-world and charming, and the dining-room walls held several photos of large trout that had been caught in the river. There was a plaster cast of an enormous fish in a glass case, with the details of its measurements on a plaque underneath.

When we walked outside, the pipe band was beginning to assemble, and not long after it set off, pipes skirling bravely, side and base drums accompanying. It was a magnificent sight, and there are few sounds as stirring as the bagpipes.

We followed the band into the fairground which by now was alive with banners and tents and much activity as the contestants prepared themselves. The crowds too were arriving in increasing numbers.

"Look!" exclaimed Janet, pointing, "There's an Australian flag!"

Sure enough, there it was, proudly flying among many other flags. When we asked about it, we were told it was flying because an Australian was participating in one of the events.

In no time we were caught up in the excitement of the day. So much was happening: Runners and cyclers thundered around the tracks, young highland dancers were competing to the music of pipe and accordion, kilted hammer throwers, male and female, all of powerful build, were swinging and hurling, while other kilted giants were busily caber tossing throughout the day.

Apart from the field events, sideshows, rides, slides and refreshment tents were all doing a roaring trade among the thronging crowds. We ate a bag of hot chips as we moved around, completely fascinated by the spectacle, colour and excitement that takes place each year at Halkirk.

"Look!" exclaimed Janet again, "There's John and Pauline over there!"

"Which John and Pauline?" I asked.

It was a fact that in our church community there were two married couples whose names were John and Pauline.

"John and Pauline who have the B&B," Janet informed me.

John was a retired RAF pilot and Pauline a registered nurse. When they moved to Caithness they established a handsome B&B, set in a lovely garden. We caught their eye and had a cup of tea and a scone with them in the refreshment tent.

"Well," said John as we looked at the sun streaming in through the tent- opening, "no one can complain about the weather – what a lovely day!" And it was: mild and still and sunny. The organisers must have been overjoyed, for Scotland's weather is known to be unpredictable. Someone once told me that everyone in Scotland knows when it's summer – the rain gets warmer. It was not something anyone would have been able to say that day, when Halkirk held its annual Highland Games.

When we came home, the music of the pipes was still in me. I was preparing for the following day's services but found it hard to concentrate. Niggling at the back of my mind was a memory of my days as a side drummer in the Leeton pipe band. When my friend Mac and I had approached Don Anderson, the pipe major, about joining the band, he'd shaken his head. "Sorry, boys," he'd told us; "there aren't any positions left for pipers, but we could fit you in if you'd like to learn the side drum." Much as we wanted to learn the pipes, we settled for the drums and joined as side drummers. In time and with much practising, Mac became a fine side-drummer. His three-pace rolls were perfect. In time and with much practising, my three-pace rolls still sounded like a child shaking a wooden rattle. My mother couldn't stand it and sent me down to the back paddock to practice. Don the pipe major acknowledged I had a problem regarding dexterity but kindly let me stay on.

They were wonderful days. It seemed half the Leeton pipe band was made up of members of St Andrew's Presbyterian Church Leeton.

I am certain that if someone had suggested to me back then that a time would come when I would officiate in Leeton at the funeral of dear old Jim Anderson, the drum major, I would have been astonished – but no less so than Jim, an elder of the Kirk. The name, Lachlan Ness and 'future minister of the church' in those years did not occur to rational minds.

And so with Mac, "Hambones" and many other friends of our age, we spent many a happy day in the Leeton Pipe Band.

Now, many years later, I still love the pipes and drums, and that evening a little poem had dropped unannounced into my head. I knew I would have little peace until it was on the desk before me, so I wrote it down:

> Brave music of Scotland!
> It sounds through each glen,
> By banks and by braes,
> By strath and by ben.
>
> For lament and for pibroch
> O how my heart longs,
> For the skirl of the pipes,
> For sweet Celtic songs.
>
> The wild Shetland fiddle
> In the lovely North Isles
> Plays on the heart,
> And tears become smiles.
>
> My heart is a compass
> That points to the north,
> To highlands and islands,
> It's calling me forth.
>
> And so I must leave you,
> I cannot here stay,
> The pipes are a'calling
> And I must away.

As a poem it was no great shakes but at least it let me get on with the job at hand.

During the week Janet showed me an advertisement for the coming Highland Games at Mey the following Saturday, which as usual would be attended by Prince Charles and his wife Camilla.

"We had such a wonderful day at Halkirk," Janet said. "I'd love to go to the Games at Mey."

I nodded. "Well, if I don't have anything on that day, maybe we can."

We'd been to Mey several times, for it isn't very far from John o' Groats, along the coast towards Thurso. It is a little village after which the castle, which is close by, is named. A little further on is the village of Canisbay with its picturesque Church of Scotland church, where the Queen Mother used to worship when in residence at the castle. We'd visited the church, which is open in summer for visitors.

When the day came, however, we decided against going to the Mey Highland Games. Arriving at the decision was not hard to make.

Not only was it cold; it rained heavily all day.

Chapter 41

The Duke of Kent's plane crash

One morning in late August the phone in the manse rang and when I answered it I received an unusual request.

"Good morning," the voice said, "you haven't met me, but my name is George Bethune, from Dunbeath. I'm calling to ask if you would be prepared to conduct a service – a rather unusual sort of a service."

"What sort of service?" I asked warily.

"It's a memorial service. Can you spare five or ten minutes?" I could, and sat down.

"Here's the background," George commenced.

"On the 25th of August, 1942 (wartime of course) shortly after 1.30pm, "a RAF Sunderland flying boat, M for Mother with an Australian pilot and 14 other crew members, crashed into a hillside in heavy fog near Dunbeath, in an area known as Eagle's Rock. Fourteen of the fifteen were killed instantly. The tail gunner was catapulted clear when the aircraft flipped, and survived, although badly burnt.

My father," continued George, "was one of the first on the scene. People in the district had heard the crash and the explosion but had quite a job, finding the aircraft in the remote hills and in the heavy fog. It took hours, but finally they found it.

When they were examining the bodies, looking for possible survivors, someone exclaimed in horror "I cannae believe it – here's the king!"

The body turned out to be, not the king's, but the king's brother, the Duke of Kent. He was on some sort of a secret mission, but all that has been cloaked in secrecy to this very day. It seems he closely resembled his brother, King George 6th. No one is quite sure where the aircraft was heading, but it is thought Iceland. The tail gunner was sworn to secrecy and carried what he knew to the grave a few years ago.

At the time the aircraft hit the hill, the propellers were set at full pitch, meaning the pilot must have suddenly spotted the hill in the dense fog. Had he had another fifty feet or so of height, he probably would have cleared it – or so it is generally believed. Instrumentation was very sparse in those days and they obviously had no idea where they were. One theory is that had come down lower than usual, looking for the sea, which is why they hit the hill.

The fact that the Duke of Kent had been killed made the story of great international interest.

In time, a memorial cross was erected at the site and each year there has been a brief service up there on the nearest Sunday to 25th August.

As the pilot was an Australian, and some others of the crew either Australian or New Zealanders, I thought it very apt that this year an Australian minister should conduct the service. Someone told me you've been in the Army, so that makes it even more fitting."

"Of course I'll conduct the service, George," I told him; "in fact it will be a great honour."

I spent the next day preparing a suitable service.

On Sunday 23 August Janet and I, carrying the superb walker's sticks made by John the shepherd, met the rest of the party of walkers, about fifteen in all, both male and female, at the Dunbeath Heritage Centre. There was a great deal of material and memorabilia concerning the crash in the Centre: newspaper clippings of the accident, bits of the ill-fated aircraft and a large map of the area in which the crash-site is located.

George Bethune, a fit-looking and bearded man hurried over to us.

"Welcome to you both!" he greeted us, shaking our hands. "Some of the ladies have made sandwiches, so after a quick bite and a cuppa we'll be on our way."

The first part of the journey was by car. We drove for a couple of miles down a lonely road before parking the vehicles and heading off on foot into the hills, led by George.

The further we went, the wilder became the country.

"I had no idea this wild country was so close to Dunbeath!" I was breathing heavily, for the country was hilly.

The ground underfoot was wet and somewhat treacherous in many places with bogs and burns hidden in the deep grass.

We climbed hills of heather and peat, heading into remoter country. Before us great, clouded hills rose to the sky, while below were valleys sheltering silvered streams. It was quite breathtakingly magnificent. We passed the quiet, lonely waters of Loch Borgue, situated high on a hill.

Walking through heather was not easy, we discovered, for it clings and does not want to let go. Our walker's sticks came into their own, and several times mine saved me from falls – once from falling into quite a deep bog.

George and a couple of others led us onwards through the trackless heather, up hills and down glens and moors of peat and long grass, until finally, high on a hill, we could see it… a large white cross.

At long last we were there. It is a tragic place – easy to see that if the pilot could have managed a few more feet, that heavily laden Sunderland, with full crew, bombs, torpedoes and depth chargers, would have cleared the top. A hundred yards from the crash site a cement slab, suitably inscribed, marks the spot where the body of the Duke of Kent was found.

As we arrived, a kilted Roy Gunn was playing his pipes. It was spine-tingling, standing on that great hill with the sad white cross before us, more hills around us, the mist and the rain wetting our faces like soft tears, while the notes of the pipes drifted down to the deep valleys below.

I had John, a former RAF pilot and member of our congregation, read out the names of the dead. Janet read Psalm 46, and I did the rest. At the end, George and I placed roses at the foot of the cross. Roy Gunn closed with the haunting lament, "Flowers of the Forest."

The benediction followed and the service, which took no more than about ten or fifteen minutes, was over.

At once backpacks were opened, and to my surprise, bottles of whisky appeared and the dead were honoured with an informal toast.

Roy Gunn the piper, who was about 80 years of age, who has been playing at the site for a few years was too old to make the journey across that difficult terrain, so was brought up in an eight-wheeled, small ATV (all-terrain vehicle). It was an amazing machine and could traverse almost any terrain as well as cross rivers. The fat tyres had special treads that propel the vehicle on water – or an outboard can be fitted to it. It was ideal for the type of country we were in. It held three passengers and driver.

Janet came up to me. "Jimmy the gamekeeper who is driving the ATV has offered to take us down," she told me. I guiltily agreed after Jimmy told me he was going to go back for some of the older folk.

It was an extremely rough ride, and a couple of times I thought the ATV was going to tip over backwards up some of those hills, but finally we were back at the cars.

The ladies at the Dunbeath Heritage Centre were waiting for us with a hot cuppa and sandwiches, which was most welcome, for we were soaked.

As we drove back to Lybster I thought of those brave young men who had lost their lives in such tragic circumstances, and my thoughts drifted off to their families, and the grief they must have known. I thought of the many times I, as an army chaplain, had knocked on doors, bringing devastating news. Most tragedies, I reflected, extend well beyond the victims.

Chapter 42

Final days

I had been trying to put off any thought of leaving Latheron, but time, that ever-rolling stream, is tidal, and the tide was on the ebb, flowing quickly and inexorably towards our departure. It was now well into August.

The warm and kindly folk of the Latheron congregation, with whom we felt a deep and growing attachment, were also aware of the moving tide, and we received many invitations for meals and outings.

I wanted to stop the tide, but as King Canute had taught his flatterers a thousand years before, time and tide are not ours to stop.

Had I been eligible for a call as minister of the parish and been offered it, I think I would have accepted it, but it was not to be.

In many ways I envied Jim the Free Church man and his lovely wife Cathy. They had laboured in the one parish for the past twenty-five years and knew everyone in the district, and everyone knew them. They were much-loved by all, both within and outside the church community, for they were there for anyone who needed any help they could give.

Towards the end of our stay, Jim and Cathy invited us for one last meal with them which we accepted happily.

"Now," Cathy said as we enjoyed an after-dinner coffee, "if there is any way we can help with anything, don't forget to let us know. By the way, don't forget next Thursday, at 1.45pm to be at the school. It's your farewell service."

On Monday evening I turned up as usual to the Jabos singers' weekly practice for the coming Sunday – our final Sunday.

Half way through, Pat the organist held up her hand.

"Stop, everyone!" she called as she got up from the organ; "As you know, Lachlan and Janet are leaving on Monday. We'll miss them, I'm sure, but Lachlan, on behalf of the Jabos singers, I'd like to present you with this…"

She passed a parcel to me, and when I opened it I found a brand new, full music copy of the Church of Scotland's latest hymn book: CH4, which has most of the old hymns but many new, modern hymns and tunes.

Inside the cover, everyone had written little messages of friendship and best wishes. I was utterly delighted. I had been thinking seriously of buying one to take back to Australia, but they are expensive. Pat must have read my mind. "We knew you were thinking of buying one," she said, "so we asked Janet to make sure you didn't!" I think the messages inside meant even more than the gift of the book.

We had not forgotten the invitation from the school; in fact I was looking forward to it. I had never heard children sing like those children of Lybster school, and to hear them, even if it was at our farewell, would be a joy. Cathy would be there, for she was a teacher at the school.

During those last days we did as much visiting as possible all around the parish, to see as many as we could, and were given many lovely gifts to bring back to Australia.

On Thursday at 1.45pm we were at the Lybster school, to be farewelled by the children.

Carol, the principal, met us at the door of the Assembly Hall and escorted us in, where we saw the smiling young faces looking up at us.

All the teachers were there, including Jim's wife Cathy, who looked after the music. Two or three of the mothers were also present.

The Farewell lasted about half an hour. I was asked to tell the children again something of where we were going, and again they had question after question about Australia. Then Cathy had them sing *He's got the whole world in His hands* followed by a great favourite of mine: *Spring Chicken* for we told them it would be springtime in Australia in a few days. The children loved that song too, and practically lifted the roof off the school.

Carol asked me if I would like to offer a prayer, which I did, thanking God for the children and the marvellous school and its teachers and staff, and asking His blessing on them all in the years to come.

I was amazed each time I visited that school, for all the teachers joined the children in the Christian songs and there was a lovely air of reverence.

Two of the children came forward to present us shyly with a beautiful "Thank You" card, which had been signed by the teachers and the children, for which we thanked them all. I keep it in my study to this day.

Janet and I were asked to stand at the door of the school to shake the hand of each student as he or she left.

We came home feeling quite uplifted, but again quite sad, as our leaving time drew ever closer.

"If we do manage to get back to the parish of Latheron," I told Janet, "probably all the children will have grown up and we'll be meeting their children!"

During the week, as I walked past Eric's and Eileen's shop we were quite moved to see a big sign on the door, advertising our farewell.

The following Thursday evening the parish farewelled us in the Lybster Bowling Club. I had been nervous about it all day, but could not quite put my finger on the reason. Maybe, I told myself, it was just the thought of coming face to face with our leaving.

We walked into the bowling club, which had been gaily decorated, to find all the folk who had come to mean so much to us, waiting for us.

Pauline the session clerk came forward, smiling, with her husband, John the deacon, and gave us both a big hug, and John shook our hands warmly.

It set the tone for the whole evening – relaxed and quite informal. We looked around the cheery, well-loved faces of the folk around us, and felt at peace.

Pauline called us to order and said a few kind words. I stood with Janet beside me and responded briefly, after which everyone started on the mountain of tucker that the ladies, including Janet, had provided.

There were two presentations. I was given a handsome Caithness County tartan tie, and Janet was given a very beautiful and elegant Scottish silver brooch. She loves it, and I wear my tie with pride. It's a great tartan.

We came home, our feelings alternating between happiness and sadness.

We spent most of Saturday packing. It was a huge job, and depressing. Janet had been through the manse, making sure it was left as spotless as when we arrived.

Late on Saturday afternoon I answered a knock at the door to find Keith the policeman there. "Can't stay, Lach," he told me, "but here's a bit of interesting news concerning Addon to cheer you on your way back to Australia."

My face lit up. "He's in the nick?" Usually when Keith and I spoke, the name of the dodgy village identity crept into the conversation somehow.

Keith laughed. "Well, no – but I am free to tell you he's leaving Caithness for good. He's sold up everything. I have a feeling that the doing over the oil rig man gave him really put the frighteners on him. I think he feels he's a marked man now for anyone that he's cheated over the past few years. I can also tell you that he's leaving the country… going to Australia, I believe. Who knows? He may even be in the seat next to you on the trip back!"

I took the policeman's arm. "Please tell me you're kidding, Keith – not Australia!"

"As a matter of fact, it's true, Lach – emigrating to Australia, I believe, in a couple of months. He has relatives there. You'd better pass on to your friends and relations, and anyone else you know in Australia, not to buy Inverness Castle from a smooth-talking, pleasant-faced Scot from Caithness!"

The next day we were at Dunbeath Church for the 10.00am service.

It seemed no time since we had first met all the Dunbeath folk. We'd been to their homes, had consumed many 'wee cuppies' and eaten many a fine cake, and had enjoyed their friendship and support. The thought of leaving them was hard.

Pauline the session clerk was at the service and during the announcements told the congregation that the parish had now had a taste of having its own minister, which was a good incentive to continue seeking to call a full-time minister to the Latheron parish. In our time there I had come to value highly Pauline's wisdom, and she'd been a great sounding board for anything I didn't understand or was uncertain about.

Too soon we had left those dear folk and were at the Lybster Church.

That service too had the same element of sorrow. I'd been foolish enough to choose as the final hymn at both services *Blest Be the Tie that Binds* to the tune "Dennis" which brought tears to quite a few, and I only just managed the Benediction at the close of each service.

The story goes that the writer of the words of that hymn, Rev John Fawcett (1740-1817) was a Baptist minister in rural Yorkshire who possessed outstanding pastoral and preaching gifts.

His gifts were recognised throughout the Baptist Church and he was offered a prestigious parish in London, which he accepted.

The final sermon had been preached in his small parish and all the wagons had been loaded with the family furniture, ready to depart. He never left. Overwhelmed by the love and tears of his parishioners, he remained for the rest of his life in his small parish, on his stipend of £25.00 per annum.

It was after reflecting on the circumstances that caused him to remain that he wrote the enduring words of the hymn.

Thoughts of remaining were on my mind that day, but it was not to be. A well-known saying among Christians is Christians never say farewell for the last time but nonetheless, those earthly partings are hard.

Chapter 43

Glasgow

The little VW Golf diesel was bulging at the sides when finally we departed.

We'd been up early to pack and by some Herculean effort, had managed to get everything inside the car. Before getting into the car, we stood at the front gate and looked back at the lovely old manse that had been our home.

As I looked at it, I reflected that in a way it still had part of ourselves remaining, for it had shared our lives. It alone knew some of the secret things that had been confided to me in the study. It had sheltered us and kept us safe and warm. Some of my blood, I reflected, was bound to be in some crevice or cranny after the bee rescue incident, and there was another time, when I had sliced my hand in the bathroom.

As well, part of it was in us. We would, I knew, never forget it.

Soon, we were heading south, and as we journeyed past each little village in the parish, Janet called out, "Goodbye . . . goodbye..." and would follow the goodbye with the names of the folk we knew in that village, until the last village in the peaceful parish of Latheron was lost among the hills.

Our journey to Inverness was uneventful. We handed back the VW, clean, unmarked and with a tankful of diesel, to "EuropCars" at their office in the Thistle Hotel. The firm had been very kind to the parish in regard to the amount they'd charged for the rent of the car, and we ourselves had been very happy with the friendly service.

We had decided to travel from Inverness to Glasgow by bus, and shortly after 12.00 noon were on our way south.

The scenery on the way was glorious. We passed great hills, some with burns tumbling in white cascades down their sides, past shining lochs, and banks and braes and hills adorned with purple heather. We crossed quiet rivers and forests of stately fir, occasionally stopping at a village to pick up or set down.

Until Perth we hardly saw a house. After Perth the country flattened out. The closer to Glasgow, the heavier the traffic until in the end we were crawling along, stopping and starting in a snarl of traffic and ugly road-works. I began to feel the disquiet I've always felt in large cities.

At long last, the bus slid into the bus depot in Glasgow, from where we struggled with our luggage to a taxi rank and found a taxi.

We looked about us as our taxi made its way through the heavy traffic. After the quiet beauty of Caithness, our first impression was that Glasgow was horrible.

Our hotel was not one that could be described as luxurious, but neither was it expensive, and our room was comfortable and clean.

I'd promised Pauline the session clerk that I'd let her know when we arrived in Glasgow. A quick inspection revealed no phone in the room, and no public phone in the lobby; a fact I discovered when I asked the receptionist.

"There's no public phone here, but there is one down the street," I was told when I enquired.

Janet was resting when I went back to our room. "I'm just off to find a public phone," I told Janet; "I'll be back soon."

On the way out of the room I paused, then put on the smart woollen cap that daughter Alison had given me as a parting gift. It had proved itself on some chilly days back in Caithness.

I made my way into the street and walked for a long time, but couldn't see a public phone box anywhere. Finally I spied a policeman, so asked him

"See that wee red box aboot fifty metres in front of you sir? That's what is called a telephone box. If you walk to that, you will find a telephone inside it."

I thanked him, feeling a little foolish. "No trouble at all, sir," he replied with a grin, "we always like tae make allowances for Australians."

I chuckled as I walked off. His remark was good-natured, and if we Australians like to dish it out, then we have to be prepared to take it too.

As soon as I put the phone to my ear, I realised it was broken – no busy burring sound. I looked around for the policeman, ready for a jibe or two of my own, but he had vanished in the crowd.

After a great deal of walking, including sorties down promising looking streets, I found another phone box and made the call to Pauline.

I walked out of the booth, relieved to have informed Pauline, and was surprised to discover that I was completely lost. I had no idea where I was; whether to turn left or right. I couldn't even remember from what direction I'd come when I spotted the booth.

I wandered here, I lingered there, 'till I was fit to drop (as Banjo Paterson wrote in his famous poem, The Man from Ironbark).

I asked people. The only significant landmark I'd observed, not very long after I'd commenced the walk, was the sight of a large library.

If only I could find that, I was fairly sure I could find my way back to the hotel from there. When I'd mentioned 'library,' some had replied, "Oh – the library? You shouldn't have any trouble finding that. Just walk to . . ." Complicated directions followed that led me even further astray. It began to dawn on me just how big a city is Glasgow. I began to feel like someone who has dementia, who gets lost in his own home.

To make matters worse, when I left the hotel, I had the cost of the phone call in my pocket, but that was all. I had expected to be gone about five minutes. Even worse, I wasn't even sure of the name of our hotel.

Years before, a similar thing had happened to me on a visit to the island of Penang, in Malaysia. Somehow I'd managed to get completely lost in the city of Georgetown. Every person from whom I'd asked directions had looked at me blankly, and I'd assumed by the shrug and apologetic smile that they spoke no English. After hours of walking, I'd spotted a European couple enjoying coffee at a table outside a little Asian café. I rushed over to them. "Thank heavens I spotted you – I've been lost for hours! Can you direct me to the ferry terminal? I have to get back to the mainland!"

Dismayed, I'd noted the familiar, uncomprehending look again. The man shook his head: "Keh? No comprehendo!" (Or some similar non-English words). I'd shambled off for another hour before finding someone who could help me.

I'd been desperate then, and the same feeling was slowly engulfing me on a footpath somewhere in downtown Glasgow.

My wandering took me through a little shopping centre, and on the footpath a couple of buskers had put out their little mats. One busker was singing "Mull of Kintyre" rather mournfully to his guitar, but another had nothing but a rather fine voice and when I passed was singing the lovely old Scots song, "The Rowan Tree." I was sorry I didn't have something to give them both.

I needed to rest. My feet ached, I was tired, hungry and thirsty. There was no point in continuing along the road, so I walked back and again found myself passing through the little shopping centre and the buskers. The busker with the guitar was now singing the comic Glaswegian song about "The Barras" while the other was in the middle of "Bonnie Mary of Argyll." As I watched, a passers-by dropped some coins into the first busker's guitar case, and when I had a surreptitious look, I was amazed at the large and varied collection of coins. It occurred to me that one could almost live on his daily takings. It was a good way to earn money – far removed from mere begging. The buskers were providing a service of music and singing, and the passers-by could give or refrain from giving as they pleased. It was while those thoughts were passing through my mind that another thought, kindled by desperation, sidled in from the wings, completely unannounced and unexpected. I'd become a busker - desperate measures require desperate actions. The very thought that I was in another country where I was almost completely unknown made the decision easier. I was anonymous. The more I thought about it, the more natural seemed to be a solution that hours before would have been greeted by me with incredulous laughter.

The two buskers seemed to be so natural, so relaxed. Could I be just a fraction relaxed and natural – enough to earn a fiver or so?

I walked a respectable distance from the buskers and stood in front of a rather classy-looking antique shop. What to sing? The two buskers were singing songs of Scotland. I decided to sing a song of Australia: "Waltzing Matilda." Even the name of the song beloved by most Australians strengthened my resolve. I threw my cap before me on the footpath in front of the shop and cleared my throat... Once a Jolly Swagman... I was into the fourth line of the song when I received a none too-friendly, heavy tap on the shoulder from behind.

The song ended abruptly. I turned to find a very large man wearing a jacket with "Alistair's Antiques" on the pocket. He regarded me with a look probably equivalent to the look the squatter fixed on the swaggie in the song "Waltzing Matilda."

His message was short and blunt: "I'll give you two choices. I'll give you five pounds to go away. The alternative will not be pleasant. It won't be pleasant if you or some of your scaly friends decide to try my patience again." The voice told me he was not joking, but he held out his hand and in it was a five pound note. "Th – thank you!" I stammered.

"Use it as a down deposit on some singing lessons!" was his parting shot as he disappeared into the shop.

I didn't want to be a busker anyway. I walked back the way I'd come to where I'd seen a main road, and not far along, a bus stop. I didn't have to wait too long for a bus. "Excuse me," I asked the driver, would you be able to tell me where I can find the library?"

"I take it you mean the Mitchell Library?"

I was about to retort "Very funny!" thinking he was referring to the big Mitchell library in Sydney Australia, but a look at his face told me he was not having a joke at my expense. "Is that the big one?"

"Aye, it's very big. It's the main library in Glasgow."

I regarded him happily. "That's the one!"

"We go past the library," that wonderful driver told me.

It was quite a long time before the driver waved to indicate the stop was approaching. How I came to walk so far from the hotel is still a mystery to me, but the Mitchell Library in Glasgow will remain in my memory as one its most endearing sights. From the library I made my way back, recognising some landmarks and finally, three hours after leaving, I tottered into our hotel room and collapsed into a chair. Janet, who after many years of marriage, knows I have a penchant for getting into trouble of various sorts without even trying, was getting a bit panicky. "Where have you been?" she kept asking me; "I thought you were going for about five minutes! I was getting really worried."

I told her the story. She was not surprised.

Time and again I have discovered that the Scots (by and large) have an unusual way of giving directions. It may be that Australians, from the opposite end of the earth, simply interpret instructions differently. It may be an over-supply of information. Even the young woman at the hotel counter, who gave us a map of Glasgow and marked the position of the hotel on it, marked it on the wrong end of the street, so when we left it to go for a walk, following the map, we walked into the wrong street and were utterly confused.

Sadly, I have no reason either to boast or cast stones. I failed map reading in my direct entry officer training course when I joined the Army as a chaplain, and there is an old adage among soldiers: "If you want to get lost, hand the map to an officer."

The following day we went for a wander, and discovered some of Glasgow's beautiful buildings. Among them are St Columba's Church, where Gaelic services are held, and also St Stephen's, with a steeple that seemed to touch the clouds scudding high above.

"That's making me dizzy!" Janet said, peering up. "It looks as if the steeple is moving but of course it's stationary and it's the clouds that are moving."

What a nice little sermon illustration, I thought. It was St James who wrote "What is your life? You are a mist that appears for a little while and then vanishes away" (James 4:14) while God is the same yesterday, today and forever. (Hebrews 13:8).

St Stephen's was open, so we walked in and were met by two charming ladies, who showed us around the lovely interior. There is also a bright and airy café attached to the church, so we went in for a coffee. While we were enjoying it, the minister, Rev Peter Gardner and his assistant, Sandy Forsyth, wandered in, learned who we were and introduced themselves. They were very welcoming and friendly, and we said we hoped to see them the following Sunday.

Next, we walked to the magnificent Mitchell Library. I'd been keen to see it after the bus driver had mentioned the name, for the Mitchell library in Sydney is also a landmark. The Mitchell Library Glasgow has beautiful Victorian architecture. It is impressive, and huge. It also had free internet access for its members, and it cost us nothing to join, so of course I joined.

"I'm becoming a library card collector," I remarked to Janet as I examined my new card. "I am now a card carrying member of the Wick Highlands library, Glasgow library and Shetland library!"

Our next job was to make arrangements for the sending of our luggage back to Australia through a firm called Transglobal Express Couriers. Compared to any other firm we'd spoken to, they were wonderfully reasonable. Because of all the extras we'd bought, as well as the gifts, we were heavily overweight, luggage-wise. Transglobal Express took the worry off our hands.

Back at our room in the hotel, Janet pulled a couple of tickets out of her bag. "Today's Tuesday," she said, "and Alan and Pat gave us tickets to the Edinburgh Tattoo tomorrow so let's think about getting to Edinburgh."

Chapter 44

Edinburgh and the Tattoo

Next morning we were up very early, because we had to take all our bags from the hotel and book them into the Glasgow bus station, to be held overnight. We couldn't leave them at the hotel.

We boarded a bus for Edinburgh, and to our surprise were there in not much over an hour. Most Australians are used to travelling longer distances to get anywhere, and I hadn't realised how short the distance between Glasgow and "Auld Reekie," which is one name given to Edinburgh.

A taxi took us to our hotel just off the Royal Mile. As soon as we were settled in, we went for a walk. We'd been to Edinburgh some years before, but it was good to walk its narrow, cobbled streets again. As we entered the Royal Mile, we were confronted by a teeming horde of people beyond number, stretching away out of sight. As we moved further along, we heard just about every language under the sun. Edinburgh at that time of the year was a veritable Babel. (Genesis 11:9).

We discovered that it was not only the month of the Military Tattoo; it was also the month of the annual Edinburgh Festival.

As well as that, 2009 was also the 250th anniversary of the birth of Scotland's most famous bard, Robert Burns.

Walking along, we observed countless numbers of entertainers, all trotting their stuff in the open air, for the weather was fine… jugglers a-juggling comedians entertaining, sword swallowers a-swallowing, beggars a-begging, pipers a-piping, street painters a-painting, and much more. One fellow was standing on his head, which was enclosed in a bucket. The Church was there too, for I saw a couple of open air evangelists, and spoke to them, and took their photo. I said to Janet, "We ain't got nuthin' like this, back in Dead Dawg Creek Australia."

We stood and stared in wonder, mouths agape, like the Irishman from the mountains of Mourne who went to London, and sang of it.

I was keen to go to the Church of Scotland head office, 121 George Street, to see what was there, and also to browse again in the Church Store where all things pertaining to clergy and items clerical could be obtained, from books to raiment. It was just over eleven years before that Rev Jim Reid and I were there, and both of us purchased a clerical shirt from a "half price" display. I still have mine.

This time we discovered that the church stores shop is no longer there ("all done online these days," we were told), so spent the rest of the day exploring the central part of old Edinburgh. We walked for miles and miles and in our travels discovered the new Scottish Parliament House, from where one can see the lovely, elegant towers of Holyrood castle.

At 8.15pm Janet said, "It's time we were off to the Tattoo." We set off back into the Royal Mile and made our way up towards Edinburgh Castle, where we found ourselves part of a living, breathing, multi-coloured conveyor belt, edging its way into the castle grounds, amid an air of great excitement. Security was tight, and all bags were examined, but finally we were in, and seated, right at the very top of the North Stand. The view was superb. The stands were all crammed with people, with views down to the central square (which at other times is the castle car park). As we waited for the Military Tattoo to start, courtesy of the generosity of the Hewsons, the MC read out several announcements. We listened idly, and then were electrified to hear "Also with us tonight are Lachlan and Janet Ness, from Australia..." Janet was beside herself. She jumped to her feet and started yelling excitedly, "Did you hear that? That's US!!" I remonstrated with her at once of course, for her poor grammar, telling her to shout "We are the ones (of whom he speaks!)" but she took no notice.

At that time we had not the faintest idea who put forward our names to the MC, but deep suspicion fell upon the heads of the Hewsons!

It wasn't until we were back in Australia that we discovered the real culprit: a piper in the Australian Federal Police Pipe Band, which was playing at the Tattoo. We were greatly amused, delighted and chuffed to hear the announcement. We know the piper's grandmother Peggy very well, and could hardly wait to tell her how much that brief message meant to us.

The Tattoo that night defies accurate description, but it was utterly enthralling. We were caught up in the atmosphere, the colour, the music, the singing, the dancing – the sheer spectacle of it all, from performers around the world. We were proud to see the Australian Federal Police Pipe Band, and listen to their brilliant performance. We knew that among them was Peggy's grandson and wished that we could have picked him out, although at the time we were unaware that he was the one who had put forward our names to be broadcast.

There were also Australian dancers who performed a dance based on Robert Burns's poem Tam o' Shanter. It was superbly done, and we enjoyed it very much.

Every performance we saw that night was special, unique, memorable – and wonder of wonders, it didn't rain, although it tried. It was nearing 11.00pm when we made our way back, again in the midst of the human conveyor belt, down the Royal Mile to our hotel.

The following morning we hurried on foot to the bus station and were on a bus heading back to Glasgow by 9.30am.

Chapter 45

"Hame & Hearth"

The Edinburgh-Glasgow bus was full, and there were no seats together, so Janet sat on one side of the aisle and I the other. I found myself seated next to a pleasant young Irish lass who was a student at Edinburgh University. She told me all about her family: skiing holidays with her family in Canada (Whistler) and other family trips to New York and other exciting destinations.

She did not know who I was, for I have learned to be coy. Some folk have a strange reaction when finding themselves seated next to a parson. There was an occasion, for instance, on the train to Newcastle, where I had a man crying on my shoulder – literally crying. It was a guilt thing I seem to recall and he decided it was confession time. Others like to ramble on about their particular philosophy of life: "I'm not religious, but..." is the usual opening line. I sit there, offering an occasional, uninterested grunt because I do not want to be involved in their ramblings.

Others have thrown me a cunning glance and come up with something like: "Now here's a question I'll bet you parsons have never thought of . . . Who made God??? Gotcha, haven't I?"

On another occasion I found myself the reluctant travelling companion of a slightly inebriated Irishman. He'd boarded the train a couple of stops before, and for some reason plonked himself in the seat beside me, despite the vacant seats scattered about the carriage. I formed the impression he wanted to chat. He told me his name was Paddy, and soon we were chatting away amicably; in fact he was such a charming fellow, even if a little under the weather, that I made the unfortunate slip of revealing my identity as a minister when he asked me what I did for a crust. It did not take long for me to realise my mistake. Paddy's face lit up. "Well, now, is dat a fact? I've been hoping to meet one of yez for some time now. Dere's a question or two I'd loik to be puttin' to you."

Ignoring my audible sigh Paddy went on, "When we die, what sort o' heavenly vehicle do you tink we'll be goin' to heaven in?"

"I didn't realise we were going on any sort of a vehicle; you mean like a bus or train or something?"

"Aye – dat's what I'm talking about."

"The Bible doesn't talk about any sort of vehicle, Paddy."

"Den are you sayin' we have to walk? I tink you'll find it's a long way."

"I don't have any idea, Paddy."

"Well, den, dat just goes to show you don't know your Bible – it's in dere plain enough, somewhere!"

"What makes you think it's in the Bible?"

"I was listenin' to one o' dem church choirs t'other day, and dey was singin' some song dat went: 'Our wonder, our transport when Jesus we see.' Dey didn't tell us what sort of transport dey was singin' about – bus, train, gospel train, aeroplane or space ship, but it must be a wonder."

"I know that hymn, Paddy. It's called "To God be the Glory.' I think 'transport' is just another word for 'rapture' or something like that."

"I don't tink you know what you're talking about!" Paddy's voice had risen a notch or two and I began to panic a little as my alcohol-fuelled travelling companion became a little belligerent: "An' you call yourself a minister?"

Suddenly I was faced with the spectre of an altercation – perhaps fisticuffs, with a drunken Irishman. It didn't look good. I glanced about me. By now we were the only two left in the carriage.

Just then the next stop was announced over the PA system. "Did he say 'Morisset?" Paddy asked and got up to leave.

I watched him, standing on the platform and looking about him as the train pulled out of Wyee...

There would be another train in an hour, which would give Paddy some time to sober up and settle down and even perhaps forget his conundrum concerning heavenly transport. The train pulled into

Fassifern some time later, and as I walked to the car park I found myself humming the old Christian song, "On the Gospel train."

Janet says she thinks I must have some sort of inner magnet that draws people like the Paddys of this world, but all the same, these days I never reveal my calling to fellow travellers.

Over the years I have learned to be quiet. Anyway, my travelling companion that day was pleasant, and the time soon passed. We collected our bags from the Glasgow bus depot and made our way back to our hotel, for our room was vacant again.

In the afternoon Janet decided to separate the entire luggage that was going with Transglobal Express Couriers and put it in one bag, ready to go. She had not long started when suddenly she exclaimed "There's a bag missing! When we picked up the bags at the bus depot Lachlan, we missed one!" It was not a long walk so I went off to fetch it. I recalled that it was a small cheap bag, like a shopping bag with a zip top that Janet had bought a couple of days earlier.

"It's blue and white striped," I told the man at the desk.

He came back a short time later. "I can't find it. Hold on – I'll look again" and disappeared. When he returned he was shaking his head. "Sorry – can't find it. If you can't find it at home, come back and I'll get the supervisor."

I wasn't too worried. I remembered that it was full of books and papers.

When I gave Janet the news she practically had hysterics. "Lachlan – that bag has all the paperwork for the courier – the most important papers of all – he can't take the bag without them!" Major panic took over.

"You also sent them on a wild goose chase," Janet informed me; "it's not a blue and white striped bag at all – it's a red and green checked bag!"

She sent me back. The man behind the counter took me back into the storage room and sure enough, he found it in two ups. He picked it up, looked at it, went pale, dropped it and stuttered, "Th – there's a bomb in there!" and started to run.

Just as he had his mouth open to yell 'BOMB – RUN!" or something similar, which would have transformed the vast Glasgow bus station into a sea of confusion and terror, I realised what it was and called "It's not a bomb!" Thankfully, he stopped to stare at me. "Well what is it then?" he demanded. He was not happy, so I told him what the object was. When we'd thrown papers and things into that cheap plastic bag, I'd discovered I'd left my cordless computer mouse out of the main bag, so threw that in, foolishly without removing the battery. When the mouse is turned upside down it emits a red, flashing light from underneath, which I suppose has something to do with what makes it operate cordlessly. I could see the flashing light through the thin plastic and it occurred to me to wonder why the battery hadn't gone flat.

I picked up the bag and opened it before the still shaking and pale-faced young man, showed him the mouse and then left hurriedly for the hotel. That's the second time I've done that. The first time was some years ago, on a small local ferry. I'd inadvertently left my lunch box on the ferry when I had disembarked. The new laws about bags left in public places had just come in. In accordance with the new rules, the ferry was evacuated, the police came and eventually the bomb squad took away my little lunch box and (I presume) blew up my cheese and pickle sandwich for I never saw it again. The folk at Stockton still talk about it.

With our baggage worries all dealt with, we had time to take in some of Glasgow's finer features and as we did so, came to have a deeper appreciation of that bustling city and its long, fascinating history. There are many magnificent buildings and interesting sites. I had wanted to visit 'The Barras" for years. It's an old fashioned market, dating back to the time when people flogged all sorts of items for sale from barrows. Now it's much more up to date, with stalls rather than barrows. We wandered around the barras, a rather down at heel part of Glasgow, but interesting nonetheless and I recalled the funny song written about The Barras. According to the song, when the Romans invaded Scotland (many years ago!) they went to the Barras in 'Glesga' (Glaswegian word for Glasgow) and swapped their swords for souvenirs and 'so they were easy beat.'

We loved the timeless elegance of "The people's palace" which is a museum of the social history of Glasgow. Behind it is a beautiful "wintergarden" containing a cafe and grounds full of tropical plants. Some of the varieties grow in our garden at Wangi.

Most impressive of all is Kelvingrove museum, which we were told is the most visited museum in Britain. The building that houses the museum is an architectural gem.

We discovered that Glasgow is a city of culture: home to the arts and music. Every week there are 137 different music and drama performances around the city. Its parks and gardens are plentiful and lovely. Outside the highlands and the islands, it has the largest Gaelic speaking population in Scotland. The grand Glasgow Cathedral (St Mungo's) dates back to the 13th century and is open to visitors daily. The Church of Scotland holds services there weekly.

We came to be quite fond of the charming and cosmopolitan city of Glasgow, with its friendly inhabitants, and all the time I was conscious of the fact that so many of my relatives are buried in Glasgow cemeteries. I am sure I have living relatives in Glasgow if I knew where to find them. On our last, brief visit to Glasgow in 1998 we found the house in Langside where my mother lived.

The following Sunday morning we went to the lovely St Stephen's church in Bath Street Glasgow, where we were made very welcome. It was an uplifting service, and afterwards we met many of the congregation over a cuppa in the hall.

It was the end of the adventure. At 6.00pm we were in a BA A319 Air Bus bound for Heathrow.

The nightmare that is Heathrow followed, but by 9.00pm however we were aboard a BA Boeing 777, Sydney bound.

We hit the tarmac at Sydney airport at 5.15am on Tuesday 1 September – first day of spring in Australia… exchanging bright yellow gorse for golden wattle.

Days soon passed… days spent with family and friends… days and nights overcoming the uncomfortable strain of jet lag.

Our amazing neighbours had watched over our house, Puddleby on Sea, and faithfully tended its lawns and shrubs. In the garden, a ripening bunch of bananas was yet another reminder that we were no longer in the far north of Scotland.

Sometimes, to this day, I have a strange sensation that those wonderful months spent in the parish of Latheron, in bonnie Caithness, were part of a lovely dream – but there are smiling faces in my dreams, and braes and burns and heather-sweet hills and people and adventures too real to be dreams.

Looking down at me from a shelf above my desk is a teddy bear, wearing a cheerful tartan bow tie, arms open in a welcome.

It was sitting on the desk in the manse at Lybster when we arrived, thoughtfully put there by one of those gracious people we have come to know and love, and it kept me company all those days, and will always do so.

Each time I look at the bear I think of them.

Epilogue

The Rev Gordon Oliver, a fine and godly minister whom I knew in Shetland, was inducted into the parish of Latheron not long after we returned to Australia and for that we thank God.

There is a degree of joy in being able to conclude a story such as this by looking back and seeing God's hand in there, and to realise that all along, the One Who promised never to leave us or forsake us is 'ever faithful, ever sure.'

On my desk as I write is one of the treasured gifts we brought back to Australia from Caithness. It's a Highland Quaich; a traditional Scottish shallow drinking cup, with a handle either side.

In olden days the Quaich was fashioned out of wood or leather or from a horn, but these days most are made of pewter, then silver-plated.

The strange name, 'Quaich' is derived from the Gaelic cuach, which means 'shallow cup' and was used as 'a cup of welcome' or offered as a farewell drink.

We'll tak' a cup o' kindness yet and quaff the farewell drink. May God bless you, this day and always.

The Banks of the Burn of the Strath of Dunbeath
O white gleams the snow on lofty Morven*,
And green grows the grass through valley and glen,
Yellow the whins* through woodland and heath,
To the banks of the burn* of the strath of Dunbeath*.

May had arrived in Bonnie Caithness*;
Gone were the may gobs* in spring's warm caress.
The sleeping earth wakened when winter was done;
Surrendered her heart in the arms of the sun.

Close by Dunbeath there's a quaint little path
Meandering down to a shade-mottled strath*.
Cant-robins* and gowans* and patches of fern
Sprinkle the banks of the bubbling burn*.

We sat on the bank, sweet Janet and I
Amid Lenten lilies* and buckie-faalie*,
And picked the wild-flowers that grew from beneath
The banks of the burn of the strath of Dunbeath.

O, how my heart longs, one day to return,
To walk once again by that sweet-flowing burn,
Where wild-flowers sprinkle - a glorious wreath -
The banks of the burn of the strath of Dunbeath.
Lachlan Ness

- ....

*Morven. Highest hill in Caithness.
*Whins: The Caithness name for gorse
*Burn: a small stream
*Dunbeath: a village in Caithness
*May gobs: The May storms
*Strath, a place between two hills.
*Caithness: NE Highlands. The most northerly mainland county in Scotland
*Cant-robins: dwarf wild roses
*Gowans: Daisies
*Lenten lilies: Daffodils
*Buckie-faalie: Primroses